Alexander Rodchenko, Melnikov on his roof terrace, 1929,

CONTENTS

A FEW PRELIMINARY REMARKS

What my eyes beheld was simultaneous,
but what I shall now write down will be successive,
because language is successive.
Borges, *The Aleph*

ARCHITECTURE IS A WEB of many different threads, interwoven, interlinked and entangled in all sorts of different ways. However, this image immediately becomes less vivid if we expand the metaphor to describe the fact that the threads frequently have very different, contradictory or even mutually exclusive characteristics and, what is more, seem to be trying to pull the whole web into all kinds of different directions. There is little more one can say, in other words, than that architecture is characterised by complex and contradictory relations and conditions that have highly divergent trends. The business of architecture, then, would be to mediate between these heterogeneous claims, requirements and components, and the work of an architect would be that of a moderator. The picture of architecture that emerges is thus of something assembled – an image that everyday experience confirms as correct.

Let us pick two basic givens from the multitude of factors which constitute architecture or by which it is determined – givens that can be expected to elucidate the situation: the fields of art and of technology, two antagonistic poles frequently mentioned in the same breath and associated with each other, within whose field of tension architecture seems to be located somewhere – or whose forces affect it in such a way that it continues to be in a more or less stable position – or is pulled back and forth between them.

However, things immediately get somewhat confused when we recall that in Greek ›art‹ is called τέχνη (technē), which can be equally well be translated as ›technology‹, so that it is probably also possible or even necessary (at least as far as their origin is concerned) to think of the two antagonists – as the ancient Greeks obviously did – as something shared, something undivided. Etymologically τέχνη is derived from the Indo-European root ›*tek‹, which means something like ›construct‹ or ›build‹ and is especially linked to the art of the carpenter; it recurs, among others, in such words as ›architect‹ and ›architecture‹. The assertion that architecture is defined in the field of tension of art and technology, that it can be located somewhere on the line between the two points, needs to be challenged in view of this background of linguistic and conceptual history.

In this context we might also question why architecture, which in its archaic derivation from construction and building helps define the once undivided field of technology and art, the point of departure for both disciplines, is now assigned a role forced into passivity, to be thought of merely as the area where the spheres of art and technology overlap.

Yet architecture could also be understood in a different way – as something that perhaps does not necessarily call for the modern separation of art and technology – or, from a radical point of view, does not even permit it.

Still, in order to be able to think about architecture, we cannot help inquiring about art and technology; as we do so, we will not refer to the origin they have in common, but actually make the dichotomy the starting point of our investigation.

It may be useful here to take a brief look at something that legitimises maybe not necessarily architecture, but definitely building – that is to say, purpose. Unlike art, ›fine‹ or ›pure‹

art, which, at least according to an idealistic view, can derive its legitimacy only from itself, the existence of a building is always rooted in something that is located outside itself. Even if the essence or the essential part of architecture remains untouched by particular purposes, the very fact that architecture has a specific purpose is the basis of its existence, and it is hardly, if at all, possible to imagine architecture without it.

Here a distinction should be made between purpose as the fundamental legitimation of architecture and additional concerns, such as certain specifications expressed by the client, or the type of concerns that could be described as the architect's inner motivation and that as a general rule drive his work far more strongly than any more or less abstractly experienced ›business of architecture‹ – such factors as environmental issues, his social responsibility, or his personal vanity, all of which may easily be left out of consideration without compromising architecture as such.

However, architecture cannot be detached from the field defined by the two poles of art and technology. As far as technology is concerned, this is evident. If architecture were to be dissociated from technology, it would no longer be linked to building and thus lose its exclusive perceptibility, quickly degenerating into a mere metaphor.

We have a more complicated situation where art is concerned. For of course building without it is not only conceivable, but seems intimately linked to the gloomy reality of what is being built every day. Indeed, hardly anything is likely to discourage most clients as successfully as the architect's genuine, sincere artistic ambition – and at the same time hardly anything is as unbearable as the insistent claim to art status that a considerable part of the more ambitious buildings shamelessly parade, nicely covering up the very fact that they lack genuinely architectonic qualities.

And here the term ›architectonic‹ makes its appearance. We hope it will prove helpful as we attempt to define what it is that actually constitutes architecture, in other words, what is at its core, thus coming closer to that which determines architecture not from its periphery, but from its inner centre. To be sure, one might object that the idealistic construction of something referred to as ›architectonic‹ is little more than a rhetorical operation whose objective is to pass off as substantial an annoying vacuum at the centre by filling it with a mere term – however, there is an indisputable advantage to reflections on what this term is all about: much that would have to be included when speaking about architecture can be left aside – the architectonic would be construed as a principle and as such be free of all the entanglements and secondary restrictions that give one such a lot to chew over when discussing the term ›architecture‹.

Let us take another look at the three givens from whose constellation architecture cannot be separated: technology, art and purpose. The latter appears a little strange in this context; it refuses to blend organically into the elegant dichotomy of τέχνη. And yet – would architecture, conceived without a purpose, or at least detached from it, still really be architecture? Or would we only then be able to regard it as pure art and it would thus be in true accordance with itself?

At all events, the architectonic could be regarded as a field that is defined by the three givens of technology, art and purpose – but also as a formative force in which the three are present, not weighted and not in the sense of a conflation or combination, but as a consistent entity, as which the individual aspects can be thought of together or into which they can be thought together, and where their contradiction is resolved.

The architectonic could then be understood as that in which art, technology and purpose are blended, merge with each other or reciprocally emerge from each other.

Here, not without good reason, we must ask ourselves whether this interpretation can be used as a guideline for an architect's work beyond the conceptual level, and if so, in what form the resulting genuinely architectonic thinking might be manifested.

The statement that the perception of architecture basically happens simultaneously will not go unchallenged, since a building is experienced as a spatially and chronologically structured sequence of impressions. And yet the statement is not incorrect: Relating to the interplay of what constitutes perception, the impression, like that of a sound, has consistent simultaneity. However, if we expand the observation by the interpretation that inevitably completes it – which cannot be thought of otherwise than as a verbalisation – then the aspects of what was seen must be put in a necessarily linear and thus successive chronological order. Something remarkable takes place at this point: The consistency of what was seen (which of course, given its mere physical existence, must basically be free of contradictions) disintegrates and becomes fragmented. Here too, conceptions with a tendency toward the classical will remain largely free of contradictions, but in other cases paradoxes, aporias and paralogisms are uncovered – not inevitably, but primarily in those architectonic structures that are designed to that end or that at least comprise such elements – in other words, in the case of architects who could be subsumed under a general, i. e., not a historical, definition of Baroque. To imagine this, try your hand at an adequate description of even simple elements from the repertory of Borromini, of Santini's Chapel of St. Anne in Panenské Břežany, which seems quite uncomplicated at first glance – or Melnikov, for that matter.

The difficulty of describing and therefore interpreting complex and possibly contradictory architecture lies in translating the architectonic into the structure predefined by language. Language and architecture, notwithstanding frequent, not entirely unfounded analogies between them, are subject to their own, completely different, rules and basic conditions. At this point our attention is drawn to the phenomenon of genuinely architectonic thought. Architectonic thought differs from linguistic thought – whose monopolistic omnipresence all too often obstructs the view of other things – not least because it is able to perceive things and connections as something simultaneous, without having to accept a necessity of grammatical order. This is more than an analogy to the impression of consistent simultaneity while experiencing architecture which we noted earlier – this simultaneity is the goal and object of designing (which has to be seen as the actual architectonic process), may it itself be structured chronologically and deal with isolated individual aspects.

Architectonic thinking is thus characterised by the fact that rather than regarding precisely this structural difference between the simultaneous nature of perception and the successive nature of the design process as a conflict, it must base and orient its strategies with that difference in mind; in other words, decisions that necessarily need to be made one at a time must be taken with the aim that there will be final simultaneous consistency that meets with and reflects the conditions of perception, and that the architectonic structure must at all times be included in the thought process as an entity that can be consistently experienced.

How this can become manifest in built structures shall be shown exemplarily by an examination of the house that Konstantin Melnikov built for himself in Moscow in the late 1920s.

KONSTANTIN MELNIKOV AND HIS HOUSE

KONSTANTIN MELNIKOV is without doubt one of the outstanding architects of the 20th century. This is despite the fact that he fell silent early, leaving behind only limited work, insufficiently publicised, and restricted almost exclusively to Moscow, the city of his birth in which he spent almost his entire life and which did not appreciate him – and which even today treats his heritage quite abominably.

Born to a family of rural origin in 1890, the fourth of five children, he grew up in humble circumstances – his father could afford only two years of schooling for him; early on, he developed a passion for drawing that his parents strongly encouraged. By a fortunate coincidence, Vladimir Chaplin, a wealthy engineer who was interested in art, became aware of his talent, took him under his wing, actively promoted him and made it possible for the fifteen-year-old to enter the Moscow School of Painting, Sculpture and Architecture, then probably the best training centre for architects in Russia. He remained there for 12 years; after concluding his general education, he initially studied painting, in which his achievements were quite considerable, and finally switched to architecture in 1914, completing his studies three years later. His training may thus be described as very sound, and not only in regard to its technical aspects; the school maintained the tradition of a somewhat austere romantic Classicism that drew upon a specifically Russian adaptation of French Revolutionary architecture and left little room for fashionable trends such as Art Nouveau. His student work, even though characterised toward the end by an increasing striving for independence, does not leave the academic sphere – it shows a solid knowledge of classical antiquity and of the Renaissance, and one may assume that he was

Melnikov in student uniform, 1910

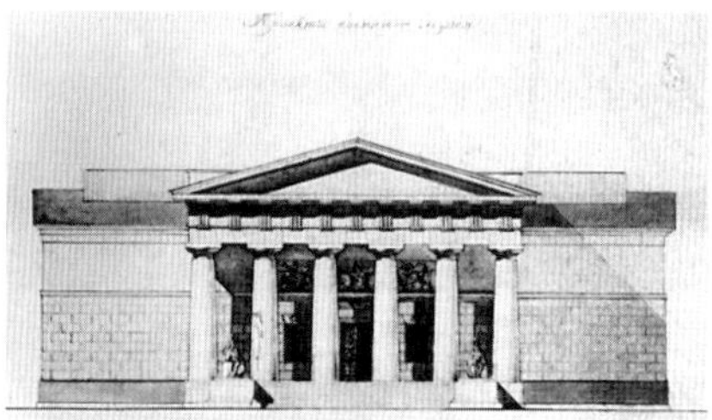

Student projects 1914, 1916

Soviet Pavilion, Exposition des Artistes Décorateurs, Paris 1925

no stranger to the architecture of the Baroque recently rehabilitated by Gurlitt and Wölfflin, as a few characteristic features of his later architecture suggest.

Certain peculiarities of the indigenous and somewhat perverse Classicism taught at the Moscow school were to remain with Melnikov throughout his career, although it is not very simple to discern them among all the architectural undertakings that occasionally border on the extravagant, celebrating novelty and differentness. Initially, however, his work is anchored in the traditional, showing no inclination toward the avant-garde tendencies that arose in Moscow beginning in 1913 at the latest.

The Revolution is the great turning point; with it a new architecture sets in with somewhat forced vehemence, and during the decade that follows the architects work with apparent enthusiasm on the formulation of an architectural language they intend to be the expression, and perhaps the midwife, of this new architecture, violently attacking each other and conducting fierce trench warfare and factional disputes. Initially, to be sure, only on paper – the consequences of war, revolution, civil war and war communism make building impossible.

By the time the situation gradually improves toward the mid-1920s, Melnikov has adopted a completely independent stance that enables him to take a position at the forefront of the young Soviet architecture. He does so not as a representative of one of the numerous schools that have sprung up like mushrooms after the Revolution, but with the greatest possible autonomy, so much so that he refuses ever to repeat himself, indeed seems to vehemently reject anything that could be associated with typification and permanent definition – his architecture is to be constantly new, a state of everlasting revolution, and something like a coherent work can be deduced at most from motifs and techniques, i.e., second-order givens, and not by means of the direct manifestations of what are extremely different buildings and designs.

His actual career as an architect begins with two temporary buildings for exhibitions, the second of which, the Soviet Pavilion at the Exposition des Artistes Décorateurs in Paris, brings him international recognition in 1925. — Exhibition buildings are a special form of building that must have been in perfect keeping with Melnikov's intentions, for nowhere else is an architecture that is basically conceived as emblematic so much at home as here, where sign and function coincide.

There follows a series of garage buildings, starting with two spectacular unrealised monumental projects for Paris and continuing with four garages in Moscow – a task that interested him not only because of the organisation and the expression of movement, for which, each time, he developed new, painstakingly ingenious concepts, but surely also because of the novelty of the whole thing and thus the fact that the project was not encumbered with typological ties.

Subsequently, within a period of only three years, he builds the impressive number of six workers' clubs. Such club houses for workers are one of the important new construction projects during the early years of the Soviet Union – in his memoirs, in 1965, Melnikov calls them the »purest of architectural themes«, which »was assigned (...) the task of satisfying the most profound aspirations of the intellectual life of the individual« and which were therefore themselves to be regarded as ›individualistic‹ objects in the overall scene of the construction of the city. They are assigned a role that can hardly be overestimated in the restructuring or construction of society, and they were destined, in combination with the development of new types of housing and of a genuinely socialistic urban space, actually to shape socialist society. That is why in addition to functional tasks they also have a vital importance as signs.

The club is thus a completely novel building type, formed at the same time as the new social order; in addition to the exhibition buildings it is both the most prominent and the most complex task for Soviet architects, not least because

Garage, Paris (P [= project, not realised]), 1925

Bakhmetevsky Garage, Moscow, 1926

Burevestnik Club, Moscow, 1927-29

Svoboda Club, Moscow, 1927-29

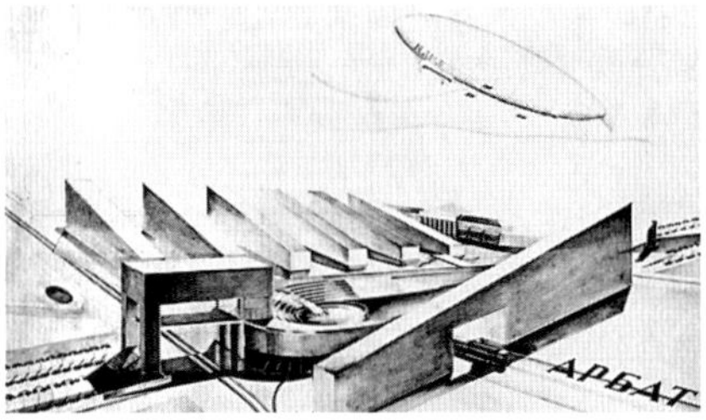

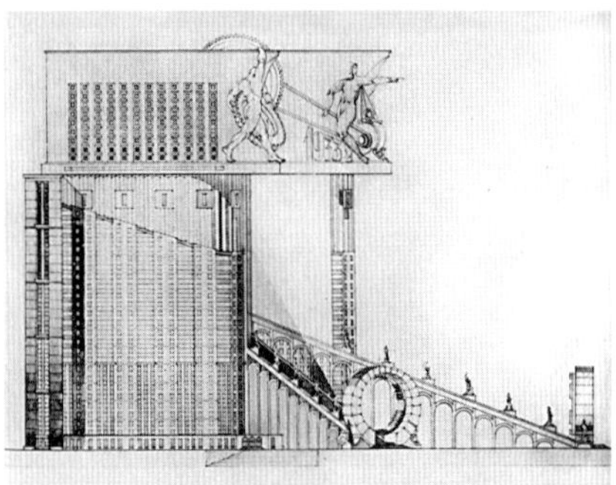

Urban development of Arbat Square, Moscow (P), 1931

Palace of Soviets, Moscow (CE [= competition entry]), 1933

Commissariat of Heavy Industry, Moscow (CE), 1934

Housing complex, Moscow (P), 1936

these projects, unlike fantastic large enterprises such as the Palace of Labor, did not have to remain limited to paper only.

During this phase of intensive work and great successes he also tackles the construction of his own home. The end of the decade finds him at the peak of his career, undisputed but not unchallenged. His mostly gigantomaniac competition designs are denied recognition, the large urban development projects he has been working on since the early 1930s remain unrealised, and as intellectual and creative freedom is increasingly restricted by Stalin, his star is on the decline – it virtually plummets. It is true that his projects in the '30s are not free from a certain affinity for the new monumentality of Stalinist architecture concepts and rhetoric, but this must probably be regarded less as obsequiousness than as the attempt to comprehend, to incorporate the new conditions and requirements in a genuinely architectonic form, and perhaps to wrest the architecture from them as it were. His ideas were not picked up until a half-century later, when, in the last decade of the Soviet Union, there was a short revival of an architecture as imaginative as it was fantastic, which is hardly conceivable without the reception of the works and, above all, the unrealised projects of Melnikov.

At first, however, he fell into obscurity. Stalin preferred a different kind of architecture and architects who could be more easily manipulated and did not crave artistic independence as much as did Melnikov. Meanwhile the downfall seems not to have been the direct doing of the dictator, but the result of enemies he made among other architects. Now he paid the price for always insisting on his independence and, in splendid isolation, systematically refusing to belong to any group: left to fend for himself, he was incapable of countering the accusations made against him, especially that of formalism, and was finally excluded from the Union of Architects in 1937, in other words, de facto banned from working.

Melnikov was 47 years old and was forced to make a living as a portrait painter and teacher. At least he was able to go on living undisturbed in his own house with his family in Moscow, something that could not be taken for granted if we remember the fate of others, for instance Meyerhold or Mandelstam. This forced inner emigration was to continue for almost four decades, during which he kept making unsuccessful efforts to pursue his rehabilitation, while also trying to stay in the public eye by submitting competition entries every now and then. On the occasion of his 75th birthday, in 1965, an exhibition of his works was finally held in Moscow, only to be closed again four days later by order of the authorities – his opponents still had sufficient influence as well as the will to exert it. Two years later the spell was broken: Melnikov was awarded an honorary doctorate and finally, in 1972 two years before his death, he received the Medal for Meritorious Architects of the People of the USSR.

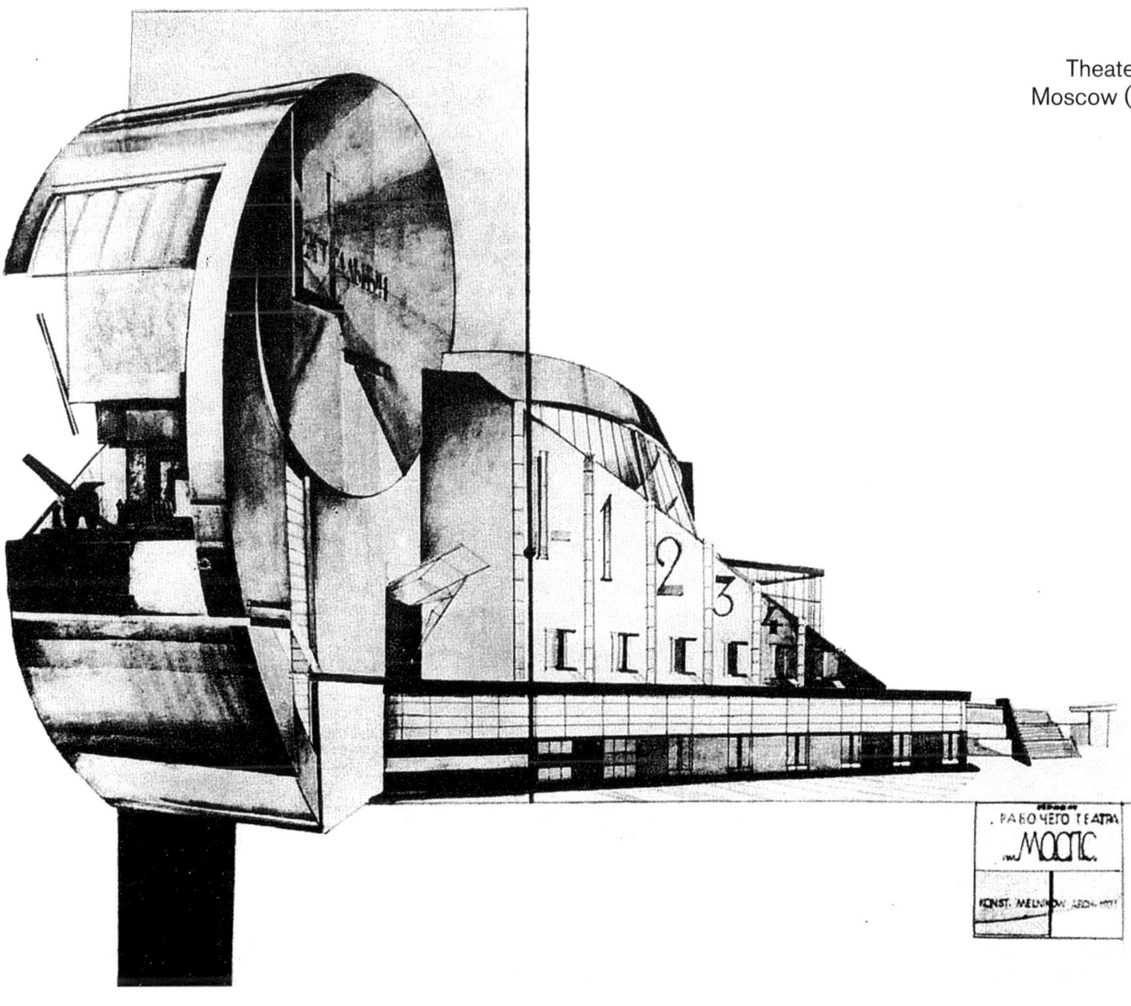

Theater MOSPS,
Moscow (CE), 1931

КОНСТАНТИН МЕЛЬНИКОВ
АРХИТЕКТОР

THE HOUSE in which he spent the last 45 years of his life is one of the most remarkable buildings left to us by 20th century architecture – and also one of the most surprising and perhaps most enigmatic. Even today, the observer feels astonished, indeed almost a little helpless at the sight of this work, and his reaction is no doubt not much different from that of a visitor at the time when the building was completed. In fact, no amount of familiarity has been able to deprive the house of its radicality, and this radicality is pervasive and intrinsic, and anything but blatant posturing.

Let us get a general idea for a start. The house is located in Moscow, not far from the Arbat, then as now a centre of urban life. It looks quite strange on its parcel of land, an unrelated solitaire in a narrow gap between buildings of an otherwise closed street frontage.

Melnikov creates his structure from two interlocked cylinders of different heights; the one closer to the street has three, the other four storeys. However, the storeys cannot be identified from the exterior: facing the street there is a window element as high as the building; with its flanking pilaster strips that – perhaps not without intention – suggest a Baroque colossal order, combined with the symmetry of the whole, it gives quite a monumental impression, accentuated by the fact that behind the overhigh windows in the upper section one can sense or, when the windows are open or illuminated, actually see a correspondingly overhigh space. This space, at least from the outside, divulges just as little of its typology as the whole structure in front of which we are standing; the window and the height evoke the image of a Baroque ballroom, yet somehow incommensurable: the impression given by the whole refuses to conform. Thus while the upper section is too high, the squat lower part seems too low to be taken for a full-fledged storey. While nothing quite seems to conform on the street side, the other views are even less likely to give a satisfactory picture, or at least one that could be brought into conformity with the familiar. What causes considerable confusion is not only the

← M. A. Ilyin, Melnikov's house viewed from the southeast, 1931.

View from the northwest, 1985

Site plan, 1927

almost violent affront against urban structures and the disconcerting form of the building, but also the incomprehensible organisation of the interior for which the outside does not provide a clue; as a result, the entire building gives an extremely bewildering impression.

As a matter of fact, the relation of the Melnikov House to its neighbourhood, to the surrounding urban space, cannot be judged without a look at one of the great urbanistic themes of the 1920s and '30s. Lissitzky, in his book *The Reconstruction of Architecture in the Soviet Union*, speaks of the problematic relation of the new buildings to the old city – not in the sense of criticizing the new architecture to be sure, but rather the insufficiency of the city and its structures, felt to be inadequate, mired in the old ways. In other words, it is necessary to create an authentic socialist cityscape. This will be both a tool and an expression of the new society and be significantly different from the traditional city, whose chief characteristic is the closed frontage, the direct expression, according to Lissitzky, of bourgeois-capitalist property conditions.

The problematic relation of the house to the surrounding area points to such contexts: every one of Melnikov's buildings is to be regarded as an experiment in this new field of socialist urban planning. His buildings organise the city as a network of new connections, by means of the new concept of the ›open street‹ – a buzzword of the times – and are thus definitely not without a relation to the texture of the city. This relation consists of the two sides of the same coin: a programmatic opposition to what currently exists, and a promise of concrete things to come.

The ›differentness‹ of his buildings was probably one of Melnikov's goals – not only as regards their individual appearance and the way they refused to be typologically defined, but also in their relation to their surroundings and to what those surroundings would lead an observer to expect. The Rusakov Club clearly illustrates this: it is true that reference is made to the orthogonal system of the adjacent streets, but by explicitly turning away the building's orientation from what the urban context suggests or seems to demand. The curved or, more accurately, the evasé structure gives the impression of being a corner building, but turns away from the very corner on which it is situated and which recommends the choice of the corresponding diagonal for the main axis of the building. Along the smaller street the ground plan does suggest a kind of façade, yet when one examines the building itself, the extremely dynamic, asymmetrical design, revealed as a complicated and paradox conglomerate of components, avoids everything one expects from a façade. Perhaps one can say that Melnikov places his buildings in direct relation to public space, renouncing explicitly a connection to the street organised by means of façades, or any mediation by the street.

The fact that he consistently avoids anything that could be associated with façades characterises Melnikov's work in general. Thus his house too does not permit the use of the term façade. Instead it has a consistent opening toward the street, the large element that extends over the entire height of the house, completely interrupting the continuity of the cylindrical wall – the very opposite of any sort of façade, which even if it is transparent is always identifiable as what is placed in front of something. Here, however, instead of its closure, what we have before us in the caesura of the wall is the consistent opening of the space.

It is due to this opening that the house extends an inviting gesture to the visitor, in distinct contrast to the basically unwelcoming impression so characteristic of cylindrical buildings.

Let us accept this invitation and go inside. Through a narrow porch we enter an anteroom that glaringly deviates not only in its form but also in its orientation from all that the exterior view led us to expect. The main room of the ground floor, the dining room, turns out to be equally remarkable, at least when we examine the ground plan. Its late-19th-century furnishings also surprise us a little when we remember that

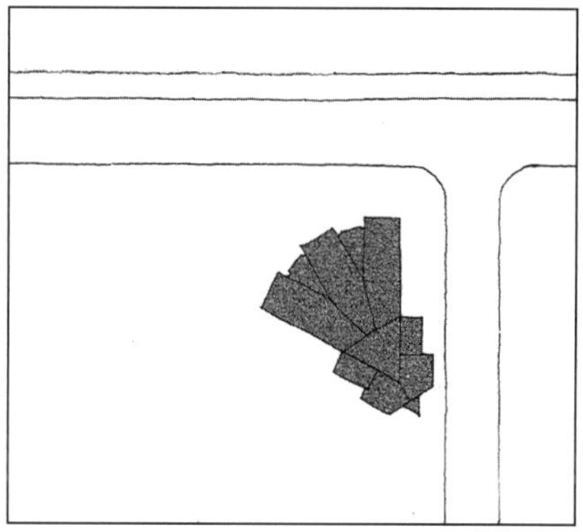

Rusakov Club, Moscow, 1927-29

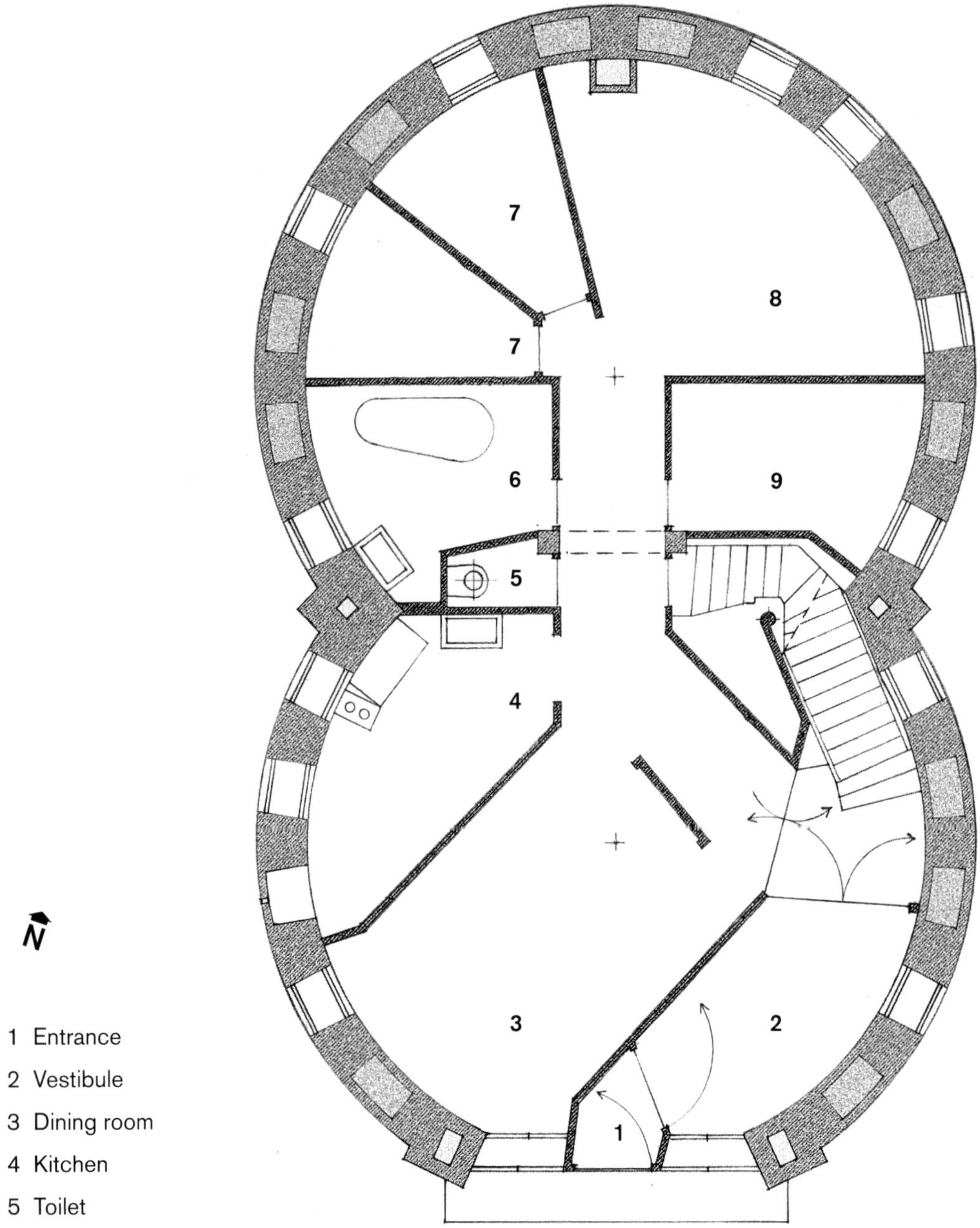

1 Entrance

2 Vestibule

3 Dining room

4 Kitchen

5 Toilet

6 Bathroom

7 Children's rooms

8 Anna Gavrilovna's room

9 Storage

we are in the home of a champion of early 20th century modernism, an architect who like virtually no other epitomises the architecture of revolution, the cult of the new. Here one might be inclined to suspect a programmatic stance, something like a critique of the dogmatism of modernism, or of modernism in general. For Melnikov always refuses to be conveniently classified, and even more to be subsumed – architecture, for him, although linked to what is contemporary, consistently refuses to accept the comfort of anything conventional and marketable, but celebrates an idealistic as well as individualistic concept of beauty – the term ›beauty‹, which we hardly dare to use any more, has for him an importance that cannot be overestimated, and he uses it frequently in his later writings as a legitimation and a goal.

The next room, the kitchen, is again somewhat difficult to understand. Its ground plan is hardly indicative of an architectural concept. The second cylinder contains the bathroom, the two rooms of the children, the room of Anna Gavrilovna, Melnikov's wife, and a storeroom. All this, one must admit, leaves us rather baffled, not only as regards the cut of the rooms, but also the access concept.

Let us then escape into the upper storeys. Even the staircase we use is not without peculiarities: it is a lopsided, ambiguous structure, apparently giving the impression that its geometry is due to external constraints rather than to autonomy. The straight flight of stairs, twisted below and winding at the top, finally leads to the cylinder of a spiral or, more accurately, a newel staircase, landing us in the living room the very moment we become aware of it.

Up to this point everything has felt narrow, labyrinthine and confined, not at all in keeping with the gesture of the outside; now, however, the almost forgotten promise of the exterior is fulfilled: we discover a grandiose room, spacious, high, filled with light, and also amazingly habitable – a room in which one is able and willing to dwell. This is also a room of overwhelming sovereignty, without any authoritarian gesture, granting its inhabitants leeway: space as a clearing or

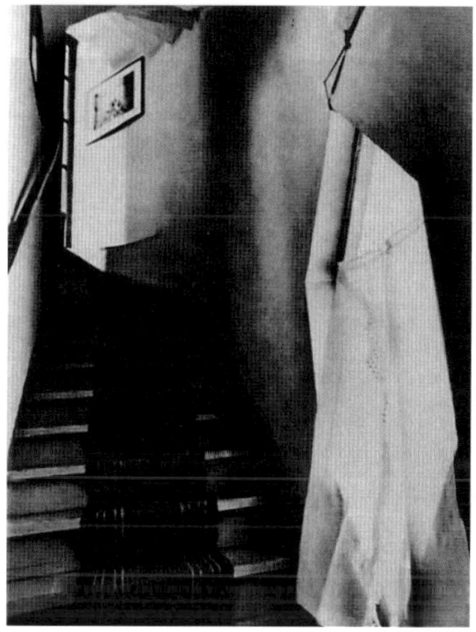

Dining room

Staircase

SECOND FLOOR 1:100

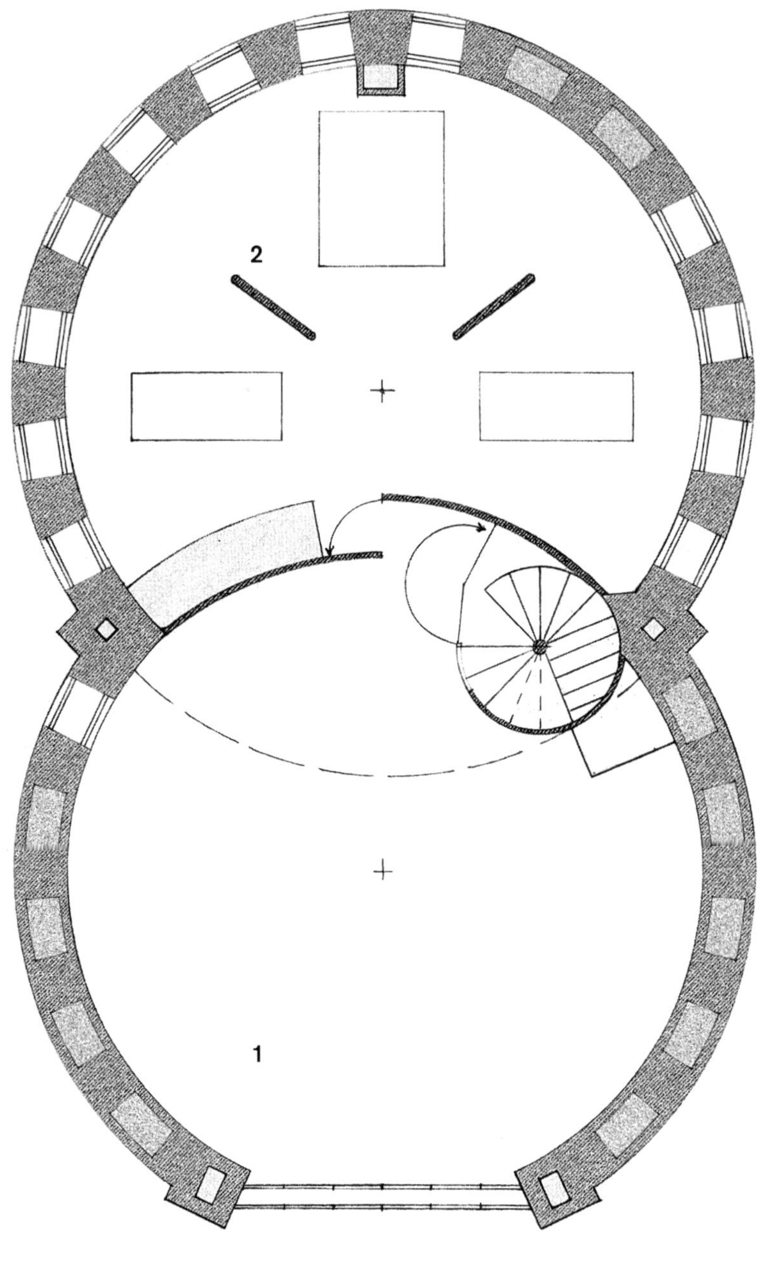

1 Living area

2 Bedroom

lighting (Lichtung), as Heidegger says in his lecture *Die Kunst und der Raum* (*Art and space*), that creates free openness for human settling and dwelling.

The bedroom is situated on the same level, in the rear cylinder. It was in this room that the beds of all the family members were located. Though this seems unusual to us, it may have been the custom in Russia; besides, one should not forget that Melnikov had spent his childhood – which according to him was a happy one – in a single room shared by the parents and five children, in the still rural outskirts of Moscow in a building called »the Hay Loft«, of which he later says that looking back on his works, the source of his individuality was clearly visible in the architecture of that building. It is not difficult to imagine, in this long vanished dwelling, the anonymous quality of peasant building traditions whose traces can be found in many places in Melnikov's work and that resonate everywhere in his house.

Living area facing south
Living area facing north
Living area facing east

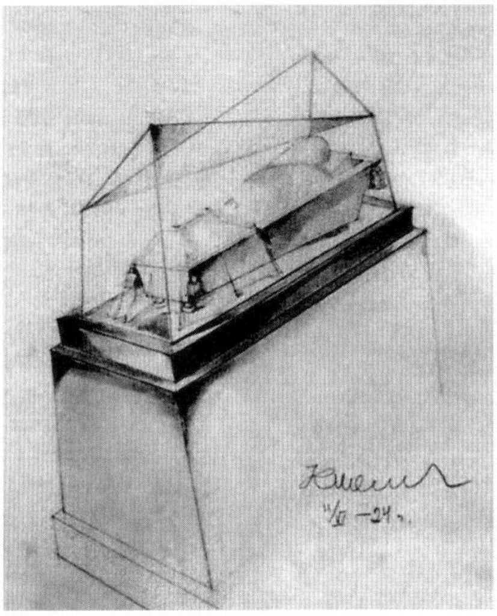

Bedroom, before 1942
Bedroom, oil sketch, 1930s
Lenin's sarcophagus, sketch, 1924

Certain peculiarities of this family bedroom deserve special mention. Melnikov's conviction that sleep has an importance so far not completely recognised grew into a veritable sleep cult that became quite esoteric. Thus it was imperative that people should sleep in dust-free rooms; accordingly all surfaces in the bedroom were carefully smoothed and polished, and all corners were rounded, which would make dusting simpler. As for the beds, they were pedestal-like objects that give the room the somewhat disturbing character of a burial chamber. Frederick Starr, in the last chapter of his comprehensive and commendable Melnikov biography makes this the starting point of a rather longwinded speculation about death and resurrection motifs that according to him run like a red thread through Melnikov's entire œuvre – ranging from his design for the Lenin sarcophagus to the garages in which the buses slept the sleep of death by night, only to be awakened refreshed to new life on the following morning. However, Starr does not put it as crudely as it sounds in this abbreviated version.

In the competition for the so-called ›Green City‹, a resort for 100,000 workers not far from Moscow, where the weary industrial worker – whose enthusiasm for the new order might be in danger of losing its great momentum, due to the fact that Stalin had recently ordered an increase in working hours – was to be restored to full productivity in an assembly-line process so to speak, Melnikov planned what he called ›sleep laboratories‹, his own invention, in which the night in particular was to be utilised for the great cause of recreation, and run-down workers were to be treated to sleep therapy sessions. All this can no doubt be seen as related to the mania for organising everything down to the last detail following the Revolution – indeed, there were serious projects to taylorise the entire daily schedule minute by minute, even private life, which was thus to be eliminated.

He planned sleep as a collective arrangement, as he had done in his house, in dormitories of 60 beds each. Everything was to be controlled and regulated »according to scientific facts«: air pressure, humidity and temperature; moreover, the purified air would be scented with balsamic perfumes and the dormitory would have a background noise of suitable sounds – the rustling of leaves and the pounding of waves, the song of nightingales, also poems specially created for this purpose, and the appropriate music: Melnikov seems to have imagined his therapy as a sort of functionalised synthesis of the arts. Moreover, the beds were to be mechanised and would thus rock the exhausted heroes of labour into a healing collective sleep. An architectural peculiarity of this sleep labs are the floors, which were not only inclined at an angle of 5° – allegedly in order to make pillows superfluous – but were also distinctly cambered across the slope line.

Melnikov imagined that this would be a way of manipulating the psyche. He was fully convinced of his method; on a panel included in his submission to the competition he wrote the admonition: »Cure through sleep and thereby alter the character!«, and added: »Anyone who thinks otherwise is sick.«

To complete the enumeration of his somewhat darker sides, let me mention that in the centre of the ›Green City‹ he conceived an ›Institute for Changing the Form of Man‹, once more his own invention and a truly cultural-revolutionary institution that should actually have sent Stalin into transports of delight, – a behavioural laboratory, a psychosocial rehabilitation camp that may not even have been unkindly meant.

With a faint shudder we leave the Melnikovs' bedroom and go upstairs to explore the topmost floor. Now it is a real spiral staircase that takes us in a rotary movement of 360° into the last room of the house, the studio. This space is basically already familiar to us – the dimensions and the geometrical layout correspond to those of the living room, and the dramaturgy, again close to late Baroque concepts, is also the same: after leaving the staircase cylinder we are standing under a low ceiling that prevents us from seeing the actual

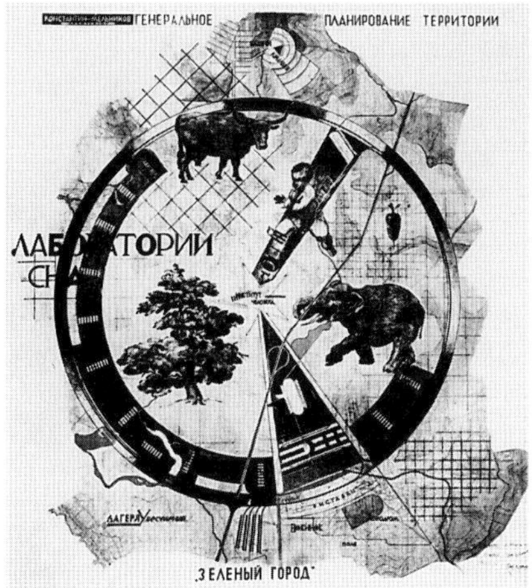

›Green City‹ (CE), general plan, 1930

SECOND FLOOR 1:100

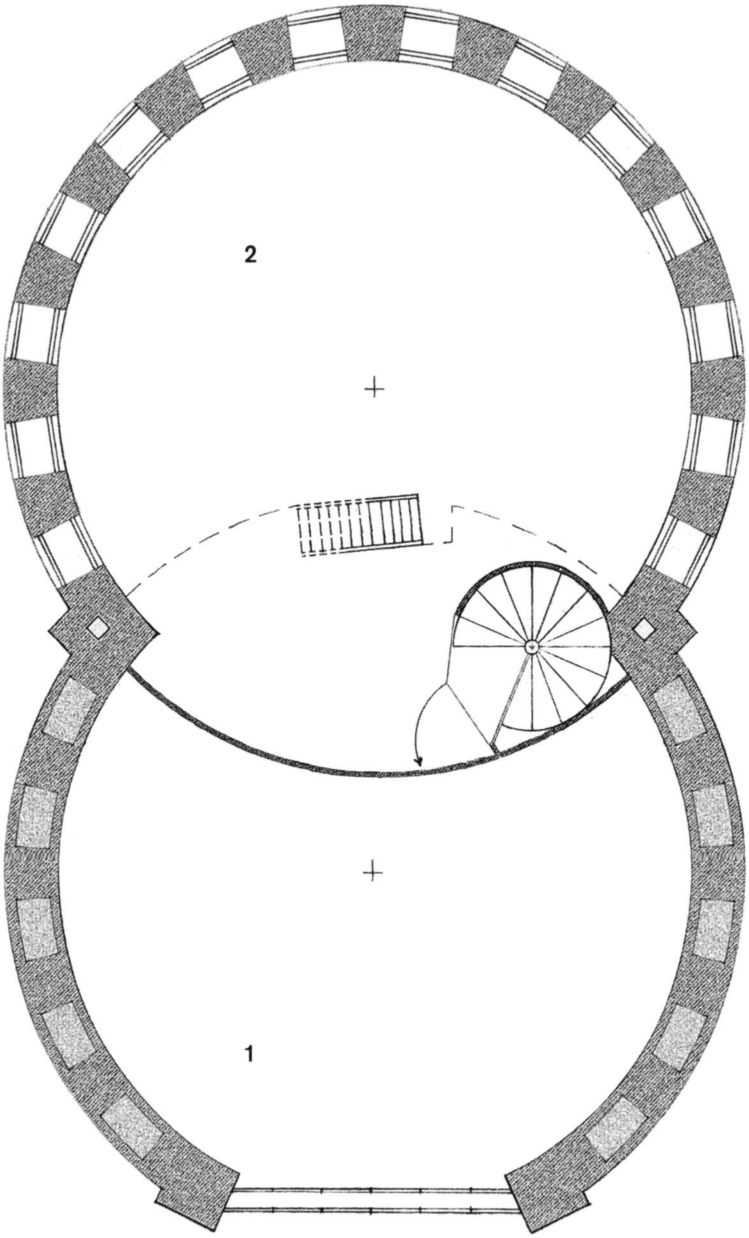

1 Air space

2 Studio

height of the room, and it is not until a couple of steps later that it all becomes clear. But what a difference! We find ourselves standing in a veritable space of light, whose wall is pierced by countless hexagonal windows (38, by the count of it), windows with an unusual shape we have already encountered occasionally as we walked through the house, but which only show their true essence here, in this apotheosis of light. What is remarkable about these windows is that their openings are not cut out of the surface, in the sense of creating the impression of an interruption of the wall's continuum. Rather, the wall has turned into a net-like structure – which, however, is true only up to a certain point, for the essence of a net lies in the tendential one-dimensionality of its links and in its multilayered structure. Here, however, the

Studio facing north
Studio facing north
Studio facing southwest, 1930s
Melnikov in the studio, ca. 1960

SECTIONAL VIEW 1:100

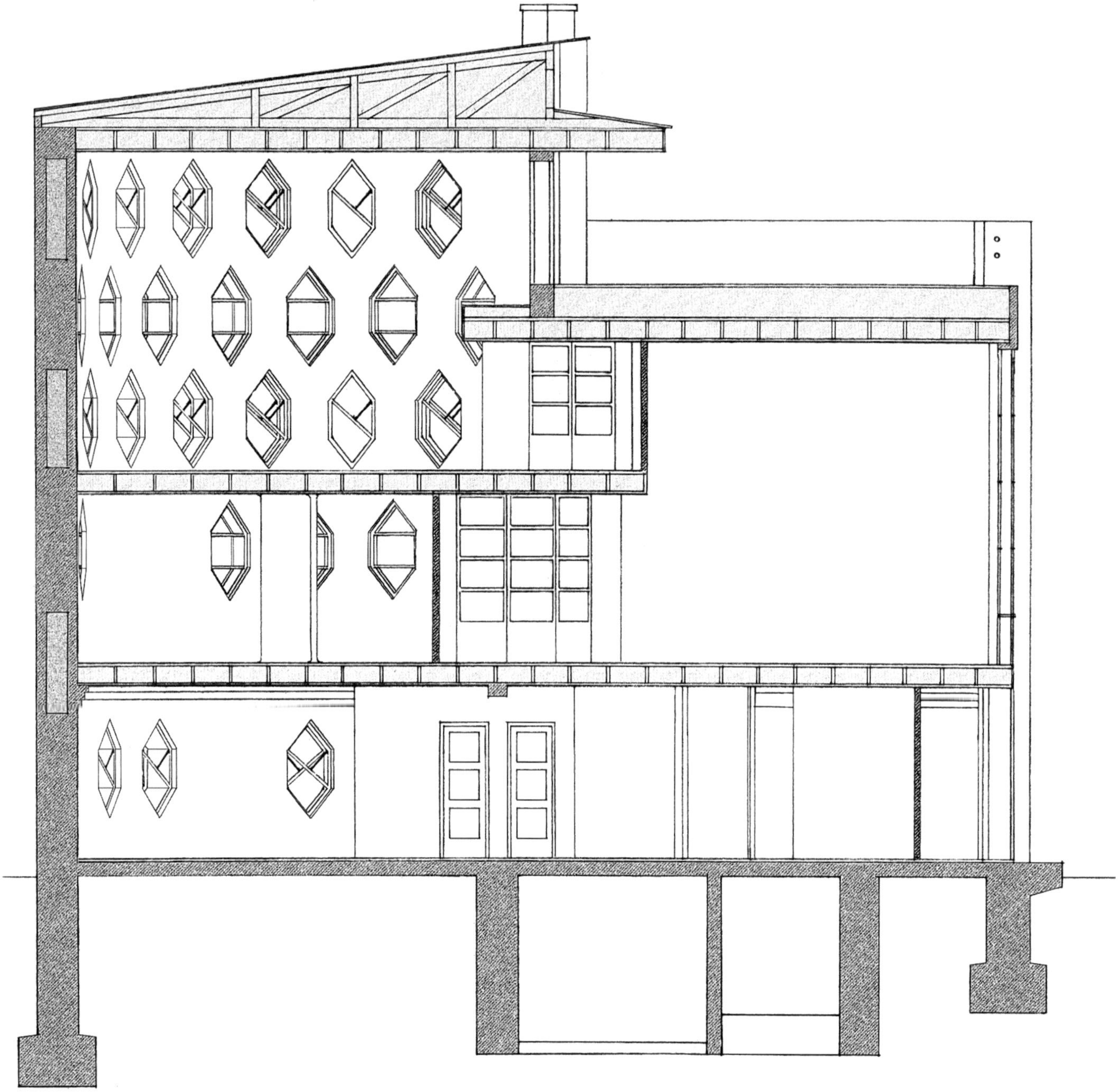

impression of a continuous surface remains – but that, too, cannot go unchallenged, for of course its appearance is perfectly massive and corporeal, due to both the emphatic, constantly visible thickness of the wall and to its curvature. Whether it is a net, a surface or a mass – it is impossible to separate the wall from its openings. Both are completely merged, they are part of one and the same structure, with both owing their existence and their form to a single operation. – Thus here in Melnikov's studio everything remains in consistent ambivalence.

For a better understanding, let me add a reference to the way the interlocking of the two cylindrical bodies is organised internally. The front cylinder contains the living area, which extends over two floors. In the rear section the one-storey family bedroom is attached to it. The studio, situated above the bedroom and identical in form and dimensions with the living area, overlaps with the latter, the overlapping space being part of the studio, so that its cylinder projects into the upper section of the living area. The staircase cylinder, distinctly smaller and exactly fitted into this overlapping area, is therefore positioned, in its lower part, in the living area, and in its upper part in the studio, thus being something like the hinge from which both rooms are suspended.

Studio facing southeast, 1930s

Melnikov's model of the first version of the house, 1927

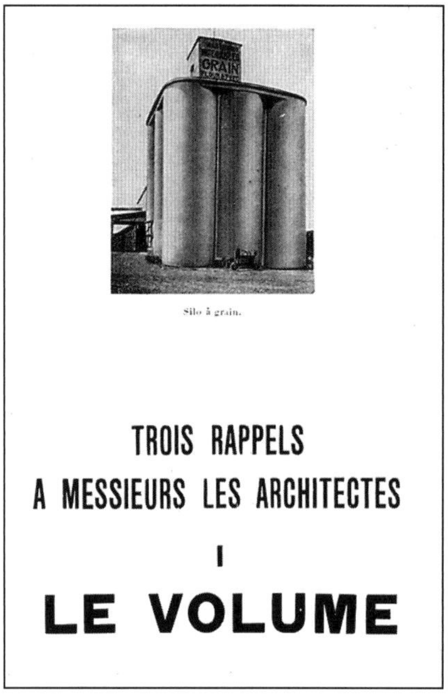

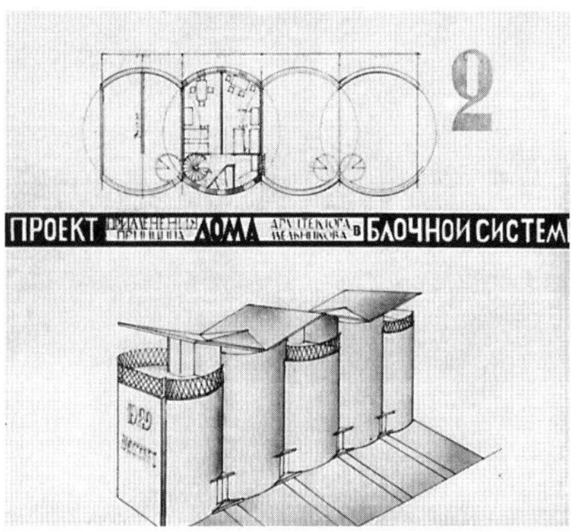

Le Corbusier, Grain elevator from *Vers une architecture*, 1923

Frunze Military Academy, Moscow (CE), 1930

Housing development (P), 1930

The whole complex sculptural-spatial composition of the Melnikov House, at least of its upper three floors, proves to be the consequence of the basically simple constellation of two overlapping cylinders. This fact, however, must not tempt us to say »How about that!« and to think everything has been conveniently solved. It's just the opposite: the amazing quality of the rooms, of their constellation and their dramaturgy is enmeshed with the geometry of the composition, is its potential, but by no means its consequence – one must probably imagine it as follows: we're dealing with genuinely architectonic thinking here, capable of handling complexity as something simultaneous and of producing the total consistency of the aesthetic structure in the process of designing and constructing.

Melnikov's preoccupation with cylinders is not limited to his house – they are a favourite element of his architecture, and here they maintain a balance between dynamism and static equilibrium. We cannot help being reminded of Le Corbusier, who in 1923, in *Vers une architecture*, sang the praises of American grain elevators. Melnikov's familiarity with this manifesto can be taken for granted, since in 1925 during his year in Paris he had made Corbusier's acquaintance and the latter had given him a tour of the new Parisian buildings for several days. Yet interest in these grain elevators among Moscow architects seems to have been strong: in 1923 Ginzburg had published an essay on this topic, and Starr records in his biography that already during Melnikov's training at the Moscow school the aesthetic qualities of such facilities were being discussed.

Related to his house Melnikov drew up three more designs that also consist of series of cylinders. One example is a public housing project dated 1930, in which the cylinders actually appear only on the outside, but have hardly any, and very definitely not a very favourable, effect on the interior in structuring space. Notwithstanding a few rather interesting features this project gives a somewhat half-hearted impression – as if it had been created, if nothing else, to take the wind out of the sails of criticism questioning the building of an individual private residence in a socialist society. Melnikov's house had been justified as an experiment of general interest, and this general interest was to be substantiated with the said housing project. This hypothesis is supported by the fact that this is one of the very few designs by Melnikov that have no defined location and are to be regarded as the development of a type, i.e., a rarity in his work, which, as we know, strictly and consistently rejects any kind of typification.

Two rows of freestanding cylinders define the competition design for the Frunze Military Academy, also dating from 1930, which even half a century later would have been considered to be somewhat avant-garde – Stirling, with his design for the Siemens headquarters in Munich very directly refers to Melnikov's work, incidentally not the only project of his in which he comes to grips with him.

Melnikov's third cylinder project is his submission to the 1927 competition for the Zuyev Club, which was also not realised. Here a series of five interlocking cylinders graduated by height occupies the elongated building site. The plan of the ground floor utilises these overlapping bodies to produce a sequence of rooms that each have completely different characteristics, while the top floors of the cylinders together create an auditorium, a combination of several similar compartments that is staggered in its height, narrow and overly long; whether the auditorium is a suitable venue for such events as plays or movies is doubtful.

Let us take a closer look. Rising above a completely regular floor plan consisting of a series of five circles there is a prismatic body that, even more clearly than the cylinders of Melnikov's private residence, does not conceal that it was inspired by American grain elevators. Melnikov now lays an inclined plane through his five cylinders and cuts them off smoothly so that they end in a single pitched roof, one of the favourite, frequently recurring elements of his architecture, to be seen in the context of his love affair with the diagonal

Zuyev Club, Moscow (CE), 1927, ground floor, section, perspective, body and space

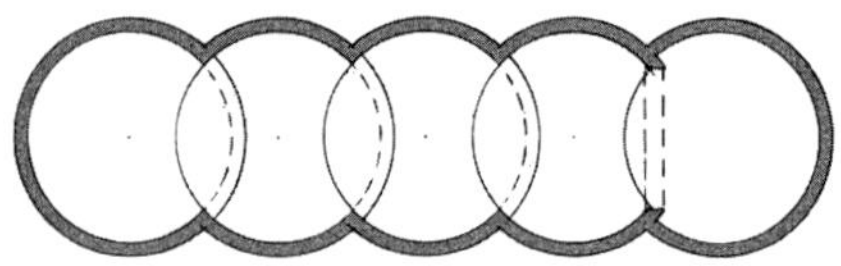

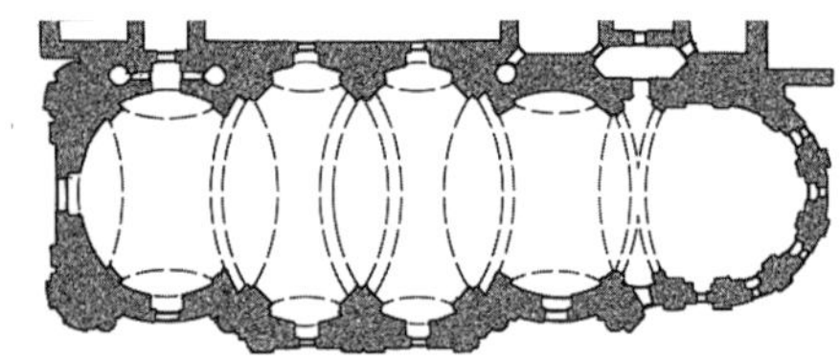

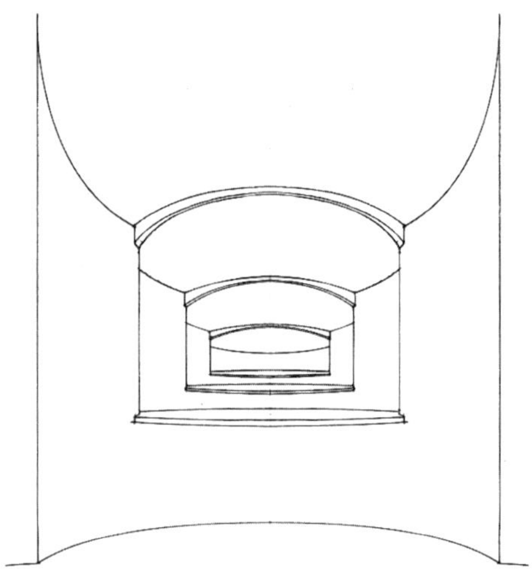

Zuyev Club, schematic ground plan of the auditorium

Christoph & Kilian Ignaz Dientzenhofer, Church of St. Margaret, Břevnov, 1708-15

Zuyev Club, perspective reconstruction of the interior

– which, in an autobiographical childhood memory, he calls »the magical fairy of my architecture«.

From this inclined plane he hangs the individual compartments of his auditorium: circular, interlocking discs increasing in height that repeat the convex-concave game of his private home, the difference being that here the individual cells are not closed off from each other, but connected by means of large openings – which is necessary, since this is an auditorium, theatre or cinema. The ground plan of this elongated room, which with its slurred cell structure is located between the two poles of hypotactic and paratactic order, has an unmistakable similarity to late Baroque concepts and ground plans – which becomes quite clear when we compare it to the Church of St. Margaret in Břevnov by Christoph and Kilian Ignaz Dientzenhofer.
The similarity to the Baroque does not stop here by any means. One characteristic particularly of the late Baroque is the elaborate treatment of central perspective techniques – they are used, if nothing else, to dissect, if not to transcend, the interior of the church into a sequence of incommensurable perceptions of space. An examination of Melnikov's Zuyev project suggests to us something very similar. If we relate the ›frames‹ between the individual cells, we obtain a wedge-shaped structure – not the visual pyramid of central perspective, but an arrangement that in the horizontal follows the ›natural‹ perspective development as it were, while in the vertical it manipulates the latter to produce an anamorphosis, thus shortening or lengthening it depending on the viewing direction. The result is not a trompe-l'œil, but rather the impression of an incommensurable space – a kind of simultaneous contrast in perspective.

Let me explain briefly. If we imagine the centrally perspective representation of an orthogonal space much like Alberti's concept, we have a vanishing point and four distance points — two on the horizon line, two on the vertical through the vanishing point. The constellation of these points follows a fixed and mathematically justifiable set of rules. This is the image of space that corresponds to our visual experience, or perhaps more accurately: our habit of seeing. One could argue that this perspective projection of a Cartesian three-dimensional frame creates the structure of perception on which our spatial seeing is based.

Melnikov's obliquely positioned wedge-shaped space is placed simultaneously over this image. The offset in depth of its verticals does not deviate from the norm, yet the result of the real decrease of the room's height is the illusion that there are four vanishing points where there should be only one, and, due to the inclined surface, their detachment from the horizon line. The consequence, then, are four distance points for the horizontal and (in our schematic diagram) eight for the vertical planes – a complex and by no means consistent construction that can without doubt exist in reality (for the space can actually be built), but that produces something contradictory by colliding with the space of central perspective we are endeavouring to create, in accordance with our habit of seeing, in the process of perception.

These arguments may seem somewhat farfetched; the perspective contradictions may simply be explained as the result of the architect's decision to choose a specific type of room, and the effect may be uncertain anyway. Yet Melnikov's work contains such a plethora of similar features that one needs to take such operations as a basic motif, closely intertwined in the conception and structure of his buildings and always to be seen in the context of his obsession with the diagonal. When we look at the façade of the Intourist Garage, designed in the mid-'30s and regrettably only partially implemented, we realise that here, with the help of the diagonal, the game of inconsistent perspectives is played in the same manner as in the Zuyev Club project, though on a flat façade relief. In both projects this game is based on two incongruous perspectives, with decidedly different effects and tendencies depending on the viewing direction.

The art of perspective, once again, has a certain affinity with Baroque concepts, for instance with Borromini's portico

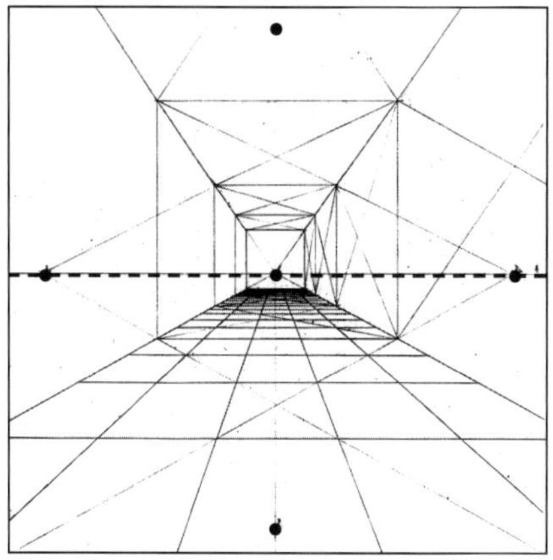

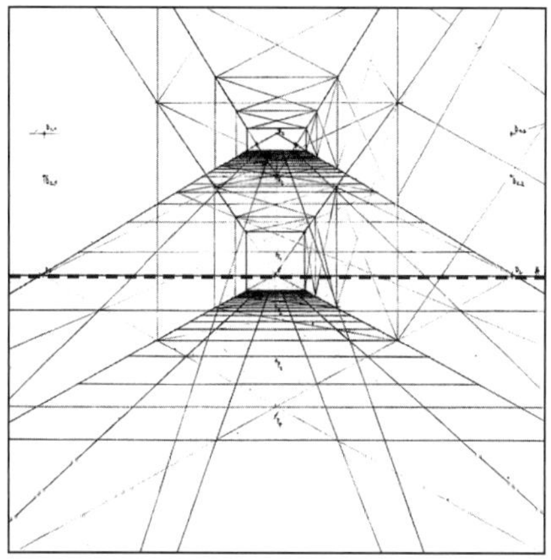

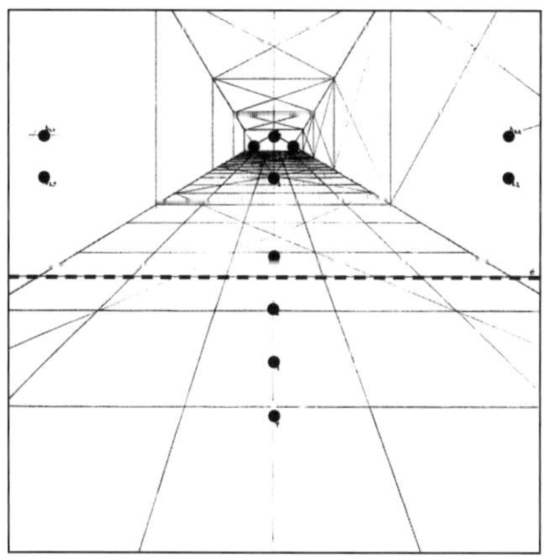

›Natural‹ perspective after Alberti

Melnikov's perspective ›simultaneous contrast‹: superimposition of ›natural‹ and manipulated perspective

Diagram of Melnikov's perspective manipulation

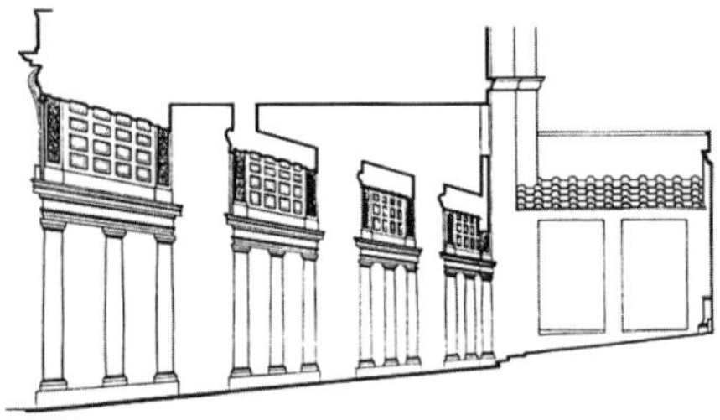

Intourist Garage, Moscow, 1934-36
view of entire project
and two photos of the façade

Francesco Borromini, portico,
Palazzo Spada, Rome, 1652

Soviet Pavilion (CE), Exposition
Internationale des Arts et Techniques
dans la Vie Moderne, Paris 1936

in the Palazzo Spada, but we must not overlook the fact that the goals are different: while Borromini's objective is to create a completely credible spatial illusion – which, however, dissolves as one observes it more thoroughly and then, as image and reality disintegrate, becomes the object of amazement and admiration – in Melnikov's work it is precisely this illusionistic point of departure that is lacking; from the start, that which is unusual and subcutaneously confusing about the building determines how we see it, and the clear separation of the perception of the image from the awareness that it is an illusion and is by no means intentional here. Still, his intention too is probably to produce astonishment and evoke admiration.

What Melnikov is doing is very similar to the studies on perception conducted by the Minimalist artists beginning in the 1960s – as exemplified by Sol Lewitt's anamorphotic murals.

The project of an exhibition pavilion for Paris, which he submitted ten years after the Zuyev Club, designed at a time when Melnikov had already fallen from grace and was struggling for recognition as desperately as vainly, brings something like an apotheosis of will-o'-the-wisp perspectives: the artificially elongated perspective of staggered arches cannot be reconciled with the ›natural‹ perspective of the unvarying widths and arch radii of the same elements, and the staggered heights of the suspended spherical caps which go in the opposite direction, as well as the ramp in the centre that runs parallel to them, contribute to this effect. Melnikov's perspective diagram shows the extraordinary dynamism of the arrangement. The alternate array of the arch elements has its share in the complex game: suggesting an oblique axis, it creates the illusion of a competing diagonal perspective – a setup resembling Walter De Maria's work *Apollo's Ecstasy*, to mention another parallel between Melnikov's designs and Minimalist concepts.

What we have here is the paradox simultaneity of the elongation and foreshortening of the visual space we regard as natural, but that is not all: we could even speak additionally of polyperspectivity, though one clearly different from that developed by Cubism: here an object is not simultaneously circled, as it were, simultaneously looked at from all sides – rather, the observer sees himself face to face with a series of most heterogeneous, actually irreconcilable, yet simultaneous, overwhelming perspectives. Melnikov's drawings, by the way, frequently present the same simultaneous plethora of irreconcilable perspectives.

This peculiar use of perspective, characteristic of buildings and drawings alike, might be described as the ›use of fractal anamorphoses to achieve a paradox polyperspectivity‹ – at least it would sound good.

Another building in Paris, which had brought Melnikov international recognition a good 10 years earlier – he was the only architect of the young Soviet Union to receive such approval –, the Soviet Pavilion at the 1925 Exposition des Artistes Décorateurs, uses similar means, though applied differently. To place this magnificent work in the context of Soviet Constructivism, as is regularly the case, is a gross misunderstanding caused by a certain superficial rationality

Walter De Maria, *Apollo's Ecstasy*, 1990 (Venice 2013)
© 2015 Estate of Walter De Maria

Soviet Pavilion, Exposition des Artistes Décorateurs, Paris 1925

and by the conspicuousness (aletheia) of the construction. However, what Melnikov achieves by means of perspective alienation or, perhaps more accurately, disconcertment, reveals an expressivity hardly to be surpassed.

He cuts in two the rectangular block with a diagonally placed staircase whose steps, to top it all, are at a confusing angle to the axis of the stairs. He gives the two wedge-shaped bodies produced in this manner reversed, slightly sloped pitched roofs, so that as you climb the stairs between the two wedges, the one on the left dips slightly, while the one on the right rises. Together with the slanted planes of the stairs this results in two simultaneous perspectives, manipulated with reversed tendencies. Consequently, the bold, angled slabs that project above the staircase alternating from right and left emerge from slightly rising or, respectively, dipping starting points, resulting in an intersection line that deviates from the axis of the stairs and thus defines an additional diagonal to the already diagonal stairway.

This differs from the habitual visual space, on creating which our perception is based; the deviation is only slight, but it is precisely this balanced minuteness, aiming exactly at the crucial point just below the threshold of awareness, that helps to bring about the manipulation successfully. Those who are being manipulated will not be able to resist.

This is where the bewildering polyperspective maze, organised by way of diagonals, is acted out and formulated – reflected even today by the fact that the few available photographs that show the stairwell, while giving a convincing impression of the drama of the highly complex installation, are unable to convey a conclusive idea of the geometric relationships.

What is the intention behind Melnikov's operations? He himself throws little light on the matter; for instance, speaking about the Paris pavilion to Starr, he talks of little more than the intensive red of the walls, by whose reflection, he says, visitors inevitably became Reds, like it or not. Doubtless his intentions were propagandistic, if nothing else –

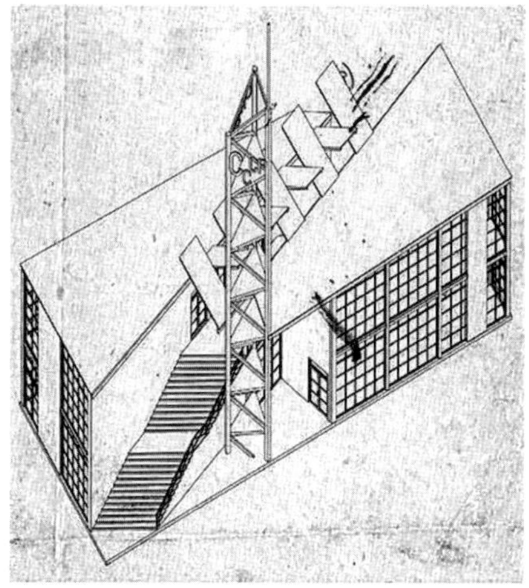

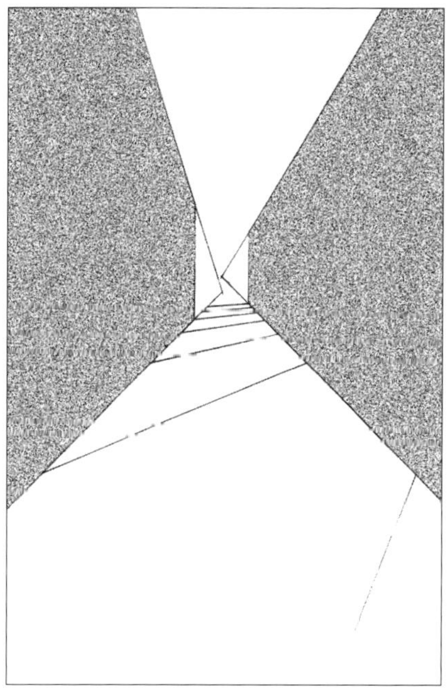

← Alexander Rodchenko, Soviet Pavilion, Paris 1925, © VG Bildkunst, Bonn, 2015.

Isometry

Diagram of perspective manipulation

Bernardo Vittone, S. Chiara, Bra, 1741

Alexander Rodchenko, Soviet Pavilion, 1925

which once more connects him to the late Baroque, when art forms and elaborate work with perspectival illusions and anamorphotic techniques are of course also closely associated with the intention to propagandise. The obvious assumption is that the Baroque does this to give the visitor of a church the impression of a space that has been transcended, as, for instance, the one consistent space is resolved into a succession of conflicting, incommensurable spatial impressions. The objective is probably to create the tangible image of an ›otherworldly‹ space, a hereafter whose three-dimensional presentability through the medium of art was intended to substantiate its reality as a higher state of being and to endow it with a secure certainty. In other words, the effect thus allegedly has a Platonic, though somewhat distorted, basis, a reference to the shadows of the allegory of the cave.

Not that we may conclude that similar means necessarily imply similar objectives – still, it cannot be denied that Melnikov's intentions are definitely akin to those of Baroque architects. No doubt he was interested in creating the impression of something totally different, something novel – a new world, which would be perceived differently than the world familiar to us, and whose tangible space would be different. In any event the feeling would be one of passionate intensity, the experience would be novel, unprecedented, magnificent, and the sense of disconcertment, the vertigo, the vortex into which the viewer is swept, would be the vehicles that would allow this novelty to unfold in all its beauty – a newness which, as Boris Groys puts it, is created by the impact of what is different [in the case of Melnikov, what was created by the revolutionary changes] on tradition and culture, and which makes this different state of being accessible, visible and comprehensible.

Melnikov's intentions cannot be reduced to the mere promotion of the new Soviet society, whose fundamental differentness was to herald the end of history. Rather, his intention was probably the aesthetic structuring of this new and different state of being. We cannot otherwise explain the originality, the intensity and the accuracy with which he explores and opens up this sphere of unconscious or half-conscious aspects of perception – something almost unparalleled in the history of architecture. We must not forget that for him architecture was something absolute, neither deducible nor in need of justification, and that he was driven, as he frequently puts it, by his unshakeable faith in architecture as art.

It takes a little imagination to get a more or less accurate idea of the effect that the Paris pavilion may have had on its visitors. If nothing else, it was probably Melnikov's intention to give observers the feeling, due to the simultaneous perspective elongation of the one and the foreshortening of the other wall flanking the staircase, that the building was palpably, yet paradoxically rotating – not only symbolically, but actually as something spatially experienced. A brief glance at the genesis of the design suggests that this is so.

I will not describe and analyse the individual phases and merely point out that the early stages appear to be strikingly different from what was done later. They are all dominated by highly dramatic circular and spiral forms and movements, spectacular structures that rise toward the sky, boldly disdaining statics and the force of gravity. The elaboration of the design translates, in several steps, the rampant fantasy of the initial idea into a building that could be realised both from a technical and an economical point of view. In its totally different, one might almost say domesticated, manifestation the building nevertheless retains the crucial motifs and elements – it transforms and probably also concentrates and disciplines them. The process that takes place during this work is a memorable one: the replacement of the physical creation of objects perceived as the protagonists of the spatial drama by a dramatisation of the process of perception itself.

While in his earlier design for the Leningradskaya Pravda building Melnikov had proposed an actually movable struc-

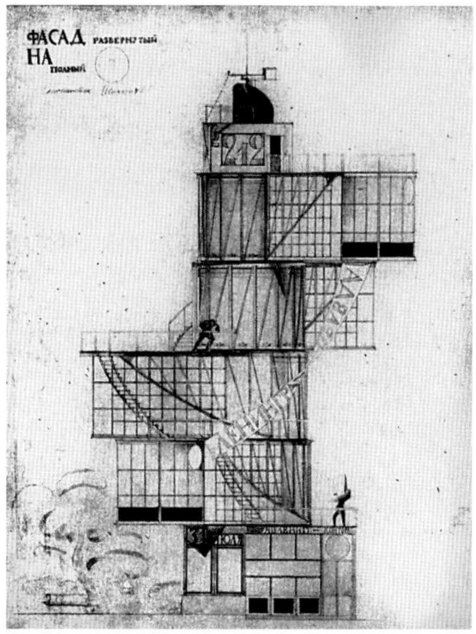

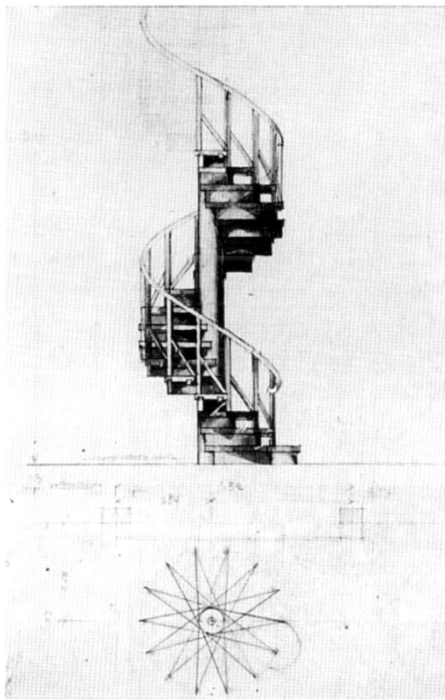

Leningradskaya Pravda Building, Moscow (CE), 1924

Machorka Pavilion, Moscow, 1923, staircase

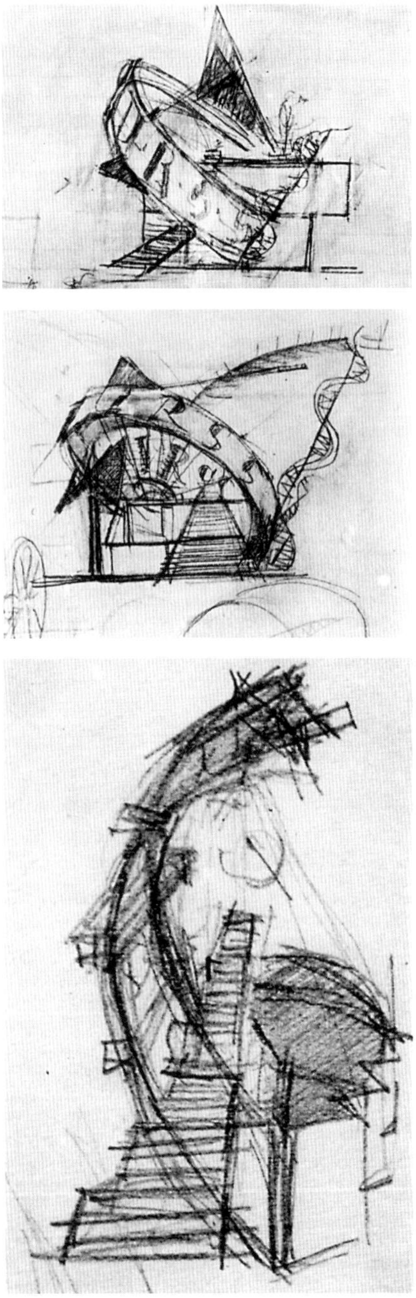

Soviet Pavilion, Paris
early versions

ture whose form and outline, thanks to the different rotational movements of the individual floors around a common axis, were to be constantly different and new (quite obviously influenced by Tatlin's cherished monument for the Third International), he now attains such fascinating variety and actual dynamism by entirely new means and a comparatively simple, static constellation, combined with a construction that is as sensible as it is economical – i.e., with a completely consistent architecture that unquestionably fulfils its task not only of displaying itself, but also of providing appropriate space for a whole series of exhibits.

A conspicuous feature of the early versions of the Paris pavilion and a direct reminiscence of Tatlin's tower and its spirals – though here Borromini's lantern of Sant'Ivo equally comes to mind – are the remarkable prominent spiral staircases that project dynamically into space as emblematic elements that have obviously been divested of their practical function – even slanting, in some versions. The spiral staircase made its first big debut in another exhibition building designed by Melnikov, built two years earlier, a simple temporary wooden structure like the Paris building: the Makhorka Pavilion, in which, at the All Russian Agricultural and Handicraft Industries Exhibition in Moscow, the products of the Soviet tobacco industry were displayed. It is not possible to examine this groundbreaking work in detail here, and I shall merely refer to the staircase, which was by no means the emergency exit that we associate with its appearance today, but the end of Melnikov's carefully designed route through the building. Stirling cites this staircase at Leicester University; that this is done with programmatic intention is demonstrated by another, far more explicit reference to Melnikov in the same building, namely to the Rusakov Club.

Melnikov's elaboration of this spiral staircase is extremely painstaking, and its construction shows sophisticated originality. Three graphic designs created within the perimeter of the pavilion which refer to a round plaque that was part of the building indicate the importance he attached to it.

In the centre of all three designs is a representation of the pavilion, in dramatic perspective foreshortening, and emphasising those traits and components that Melnikov regarded as important or characteristic. In all three the spiral staircase occupies a prominent place – in the simultaneity of the object and its representation it is a remarkable figure of rhetorical doubling, a kind of tautology we will come across in Melnikov's work several more times. The prominence of the spiral staircase is not too surprising if we bear in mind the role that dynamism, rotation, cylinders and movement play in his thinking generally. It is a conspicuous special case of stairs not only as a distinct experience of movement, but also as a significant form, and this may explain the specific attraction it had for Melnikov.

Spiral or, to be precise, newel stairs are found in his work on several occasions, though no longer in such a ›loaded‹ form; for instance, in various housing developments, in the Bakhmetevsky Garage or, more elaborate, in the Rusakov Club, where, though the design is determined by practical function, a simultaneous symbolic function definitely does not seem far-fetched: the staircase occupies centre stage and the most prominent position in the entire building, where all the perspective lines converge.

What about the staircase in his own house? The striking thing about it is that it is the only one he places in a closed cylinder, thus foregoing the perspective shifts that would have been available here. In other words, he is focusing on something else. For one, of course, the focus is on plasticity: Without this cylinder of a staircase, the magnificent sculptural-spatial composition of the living room would on the one hand lack the hinge that creates connection and cohesion for the open cylindrical space and the fragment of a cylindrical body inserted in it, and on the other hand the cylinder of the staircase, whose form is of course perceived as complete and tangible, represents the two major forms: As a model, you see before you, so to speak, the form of the space in which you are situated, and you see the inserted

Soviet Pavilion, Paris
early versions

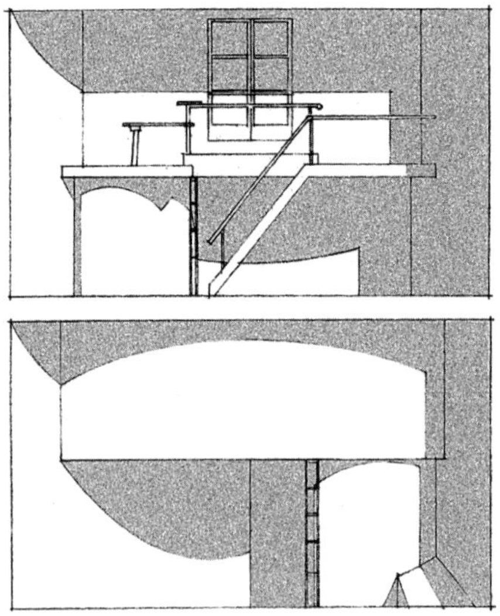

The staircase cylinder in the studio and in the living area

body fragment completed: here again, we have a kind of tautology – a questionable business in language, though not in architecture – quite the contrary. Incommensurable structures in language and architecture: Melnikov's house as a manifestation of theoretical matters.

Furthermore, the cylinder of the staircase produces pronounced asymmetry in the otherwise strictly regular arrangements, creates three-dimensional dynamism – as an element that is clearly associated with the space-defining walls and that because of its physicality and its surface basically makes possible the interplay of the rounded shapes and the few sharp lines in the light in all its luxuriance.

In an earlier version the tube of the stairs had been moved farther into the living area, outside the overlap of the two cylinders. The definitive version, whose perspective view is first found pencilled in on a drawing of this early variant, enhances a spatial puzzle that is already suggested earlier by adding the element that makes it possible to play this game in its fullness in the first place. Let me elaborate. The two main rooms of the house – the living area on the second floor and the studio on the third – prove to be both very similar and distinctly different. The most obvious difference is the way the openings to the outside are organised: in the living area as an interruption of the continuum of the wall by a floor-to-ceiling, oversized window that gives the room a clear direction, while in the studio we have as a structural feature the numerous regularly distributed hexagons that are regarded not as breaks, but as a characteristic of the wall itself – which, of course, they really are not only aesthetically, but also statically and constructionally.

Thus while the two rooms are clearly differentiated by the concept of limitation and the quality of light, their geometric disposition is almost identical and is also perceived to be so. In other words if you go up to the studio from the living area, you have the impression of standing in a similar, geometrically identical space, but in which, inexplicably, the sides seem to be transposed: on one floor the cylinder of the staircase is located on the right side, while on the other it is on the left. Initially an observer will hardly be able to tell that this is in consequence of the constellation of the two cylinders: the interior of the house actually does not allow a view of the whole that would show the entire complex, thus clarifying the constellation of the two large rooms, and a coherent picture must only be constructed from memory.

The spiral staircase has a decisive share in this puzzle: as you go upstairs you lose your sense of direction, both because of the rotary motion and because the stairs are enclosed, thus preventing you from developing a stable frame of reference through orienting yourself along the surrounding architecture. Thus your first impression of the studio will be that it is not only the same shape as the living area but also oriented the same way, though much to your bewilderment the staircase cylinder has now changed sides. Before long this illusion will be resolved, and the true circumstances will become clear – with the startling feeling that the room rotates 180°. A remarkable destabilisation takes place here, the experience of a dynamic element in a building that has a decidedly static, solid character – it is hardly possible to find anything more stable than a sturdy cylinder. This destabilisation is not unexpected; in fact, it is the endpoint and culmination of an exactly calculated spatial drama designed to be an interplay of stabilisations and destabilisations. This begins as soon as you enter the house, on the ground floor. Its ground plan initially remains incomprehensible, seems accidental, almost awkward – the impression is that ›architecture‹ only takes place on the upper floors.

Though I had a great deal of practice reading ground plans, I had serious problems with the ground floor when, in the early 1980s, I first did research on the Melnikov House – it seemed unclear to me, without a design, undisciplined. I was not alone: with a certain regularity, the shortcomings of this section are pointed out in the literature.

But when I had the good fortune of being able to visit the house in 1985, I was surprised to find none of the expected

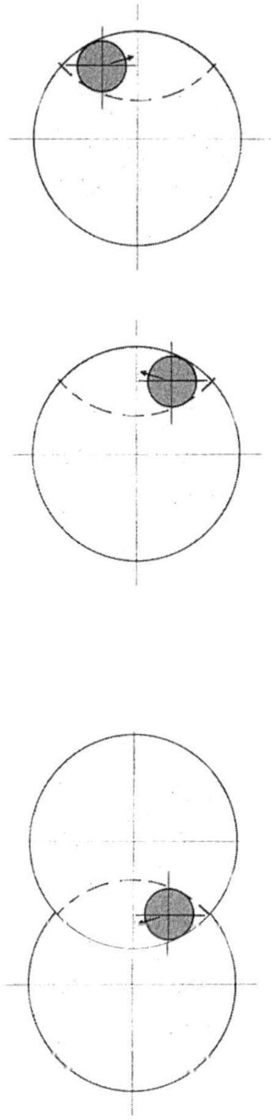

The staircase cylinder changing sides

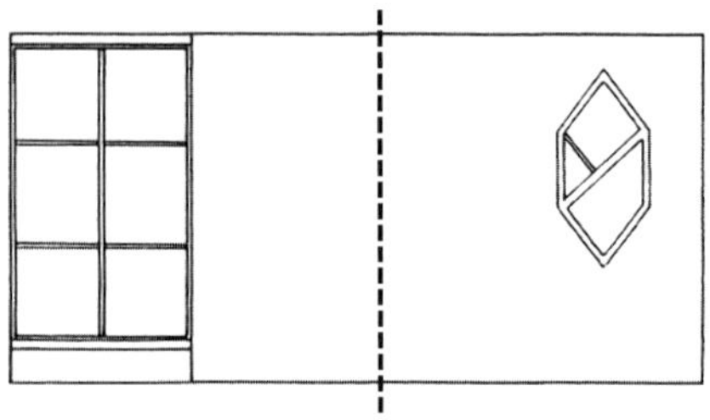

Dining room, wall and windows

lack of clarity on the ground floor, but rather the impression of unalloyed orderliness. The central dining room, in which nothing seems to be right, where not one of the angles is a right one, the two doorways do not correspond, the two windows could not be more different, and besides all the corners are frayed, where everything is crooked and lopsided, turns out to be clear and regular; there is no sign of the chaos one would be led to expect from the plans. The impression is that this is an experiment: as though the intention were to explore the essential minimum required to give the viewer the impression of order.

This becomes particularly clear when one looks at the windows: the first of them being one of the hexagons cut into the wall, the other filling a floor-to-ceiling void – and both together introducing the dichotomy of the two different light concepts of studio and living area, they are thus distinctly different not only in shape and size, but also in their definition as regards an architectonic, structural syntax. Remarkably enough, they are nevertheless perceived as equivalents (which might be due to the fact that Melnikov perhaps regarded light as a substance) and they, along with other similarly vague equivalents, help give the room stable symmetrical conditions, decisively helped by the definition of a dominant axis by the curved wall segment or fragment.

This might appear as an experiment in architectural perception psychology to study how order is established or, more accurately, how the process and the strategies of perceiving are aimed at the production of order, how viewers endeavour to force the divergent elements they find into a system that is as simple as possible and reassuringly orderly. Indeed, the process of perception seems to cling to everything that allows synchronisation with a spatial model and serves to produce regularity, following an economic pattern that registers perceptions of a similar type as equal.

The room diagram that viewers create, or rather, that the architectural constellation prompts them to create in the process of perception, is clear, stable, symmetrically ordered.

It seems quite possible that in the axial and symmetrical arrangement we can find a reminiscence of room diagrams like those with which Melnikov first became familiar during his long years of study at the Moscow School of Painting, Sculpture and Architecture as the canon of the architectural principles taught there; at the same time we must not overlook that the openings of the corners point to urbanistic concepts rather than concepts related to interiors, which is probably linked to the fact that both in the case of the former and in Melnikov's dining room the main concern is to organise comparatively complex relationships.

This brings us back to the interplay of stabilisation and destabilisation, whose dramaturgy seems to determine how we perceive the Melnikov House. At the same time, we must be aware that all this can be valid only for a first encounter – something like an initiation experience; on subsequent visits this drama will be replaced by stable conditions, and will have no importance particularly for the residents themselves. Yet this does not mean that we should regard it as a superfluous diversion – it is precisely the carefully worked-out contrast between the highly dramatic first encounter and the reassurance of later visits that constitutes a unique feature of Melnikov's architectural drama and a significant expansion of his repertory. Here it should also be noted that the dramatic staging definitely does not come at the price of relinquishing or merely reducing the building's basic durable habitability – there is hardly another house that gives one the same continuous feeling of being in the right place.

First-time visitors find themselves in front of a building whose elements, which tend to be monumental and almost somewhat histrionic, lead them to expect a clear and unambiguous axial orientation: it promises something without deception. But nothing has prepared us for what happens when we enter the building: we are in a room whose orientation most glaringly deviates from that of the building; it seems the opposite of clear, and its heterogeneous elements refuse to be used to form a stable structure.

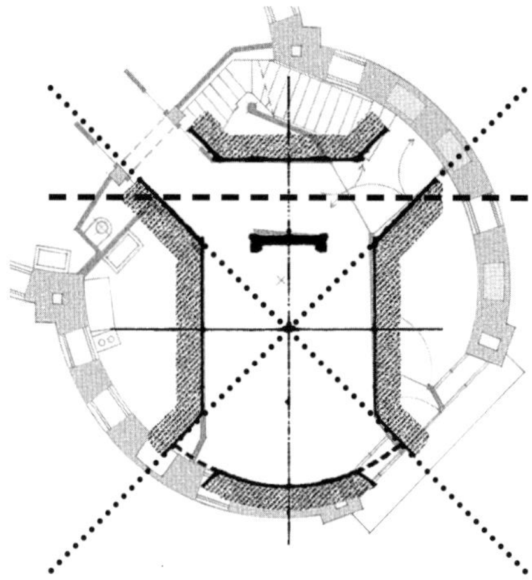

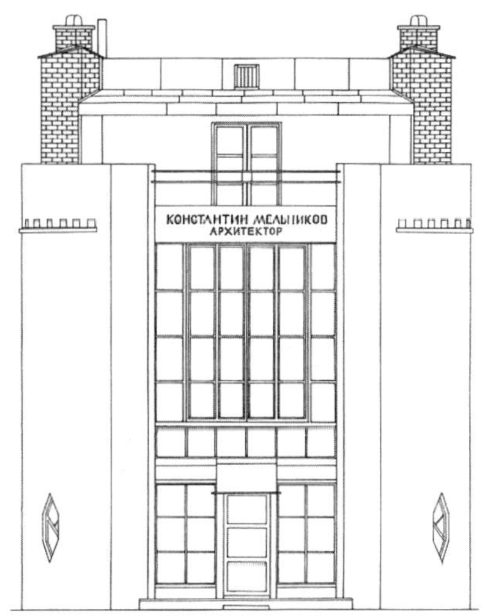

Room diagram of the dining room

View facing the street

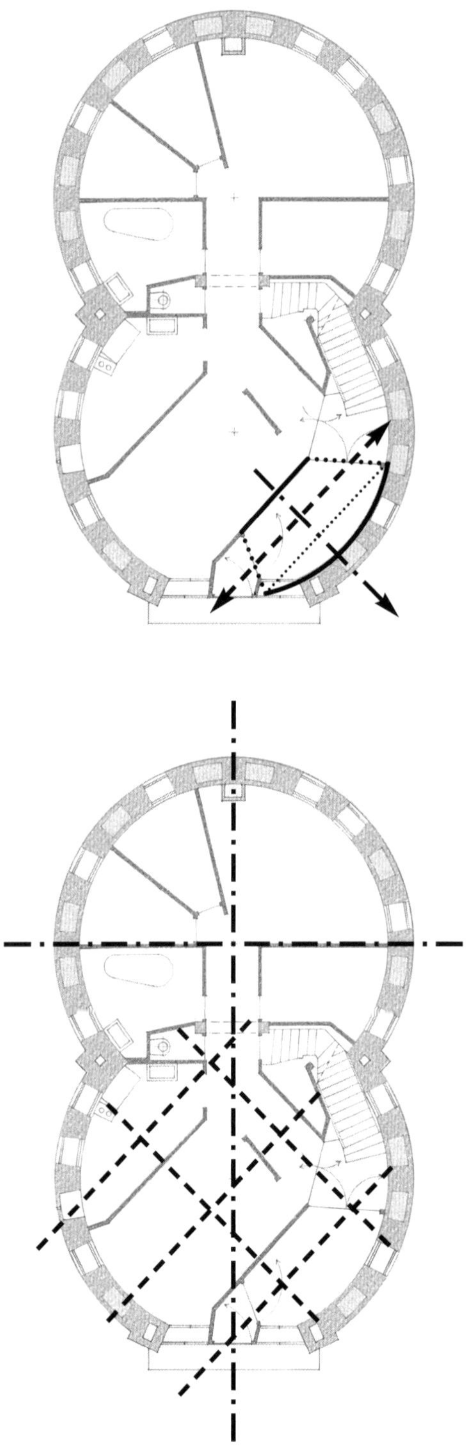

Ground floor: Dramaturgy of movement and orientation

While this is something that suggests itself when we examine the ground plan, the room that visitors perceive when they enter the house only partially fits that impression. In fact here too, as in the dining room, although there is considerable heterogeneity, the merely suggested trends are still so strong that the room may be perceived to be quite ordered and organised – in other words, not at all something random that owes its existence only to operations not intended to create its form and design.

It is the constellation of two elements that – thanks to the fact that their trends correspond – creates the order: the wall to the dining room, placed at an angle of 45° to the principal axis, and the circular segment of the exterior wall, whose chord is roughly parallel to it. Thus the combination of these two elements establishes the diagonal as the trend of the room. It is remarkable to what extent this narrow, corridor-like area actually has spatial quality, which it probably owes to the exact interplay of its two distinctly different axes: one an asymmetrically flanked line of movement, the other, at right angles to it, an ordering symmetry axis defined by the constellation of a straight and a curved wall.

A few steps later the new direction is stabilised as an orthogonal system, and as soon as we enter the dining room, any doubts about the orientation are dispelled: the diagonal is now established as the principal direction, with the help of a considerable amount of ordering measures. The stability of the new direction does not last long, however: The corridor that gives access to the rooms located in the rear cylinder again brings into play the old and actual principal direction of the building here as a renewed disruption – once more by means of a large number of elements apt to create order, such as orthogonality, axes, a marked endpoint, symmetries, and even the suggestion of a portal by means of a lintel.

Thus the interplay of destabilisation and stabilisation here is done in such a way that the features that initially caused the disruption become the basis of the new order – in which the old order in turn appears as a disruption, only to continue the game in turn with the same operation.

This is the illusory puzzle of the ground floor. Visitors who immediately go upstairs, to the large living room, will perceive their walk differently – they too are initially pushed into a diagonal movement, which then, however, is intercepted by the curved outside wall, gets sidetracked and led upstairs in a narrowing spiral line, only to end up in the closed staircase cylinder and the first steps of the spiral staircase.

In other words, although the ground plan shows it as an almost careless structure that seems clumsy and forced, making one think of amateurish and makeshift work, the staircase is an elaborate, most artfully arranged, carefully staged spatial structure – truly spatial, in three dimensions.

The gradually narrowing spiral movement that captured us earlier releases us, or rather tosses us, into the living room, a space which with its large, floor-to-ceiling window cannot hide a slight hint of classicism, including in its orientation. On the top floor – the studio – contrary to all expectations and leaving the familiar far behind, the wall dissolves in a magnificent netlike structure of light.

The time has come to take a look at the construction – something that Melnikov probably regarded as a part of his work not especially worth mentioning but taken for granted, and that he occasionally left to others, if we are to believe his statements, for instance, about the Paris pavilion. His house, however, says something quite different. In fact, it proves him to be one of the great constructors among architects, in whose works construction – though you would not easily notice it – has an originality hardly equalled in modern architecture.

To illustrate this, we must once more retrace our steps a little. Melnikov built his house in 1927/28, in the final phase of the so-called New Economic Policy (NEP), which had been proclaimed by Lenin in 1921 in order to help deal with the supply problems that had assumed dramatic proportions as a consequence of the revolution and civil war. This short

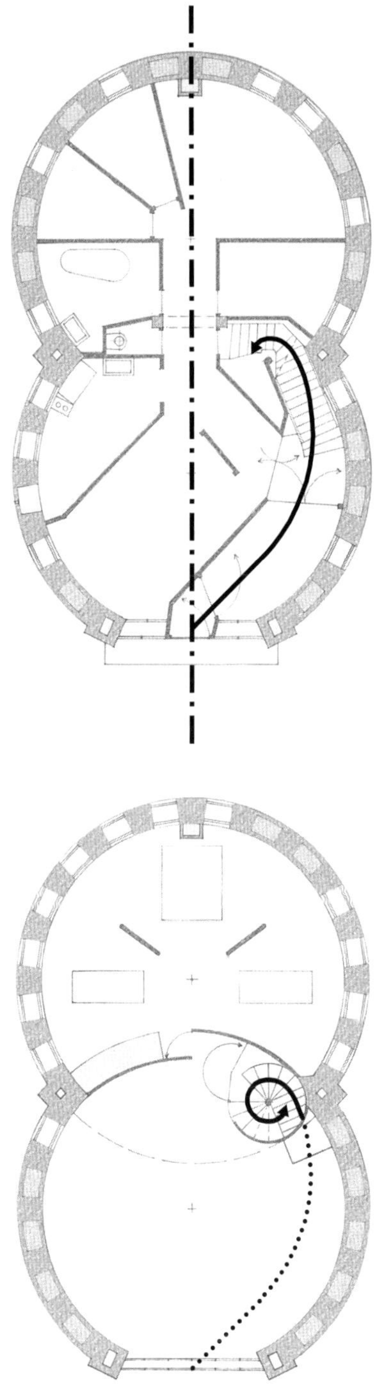

Dramaturgy of the staircase

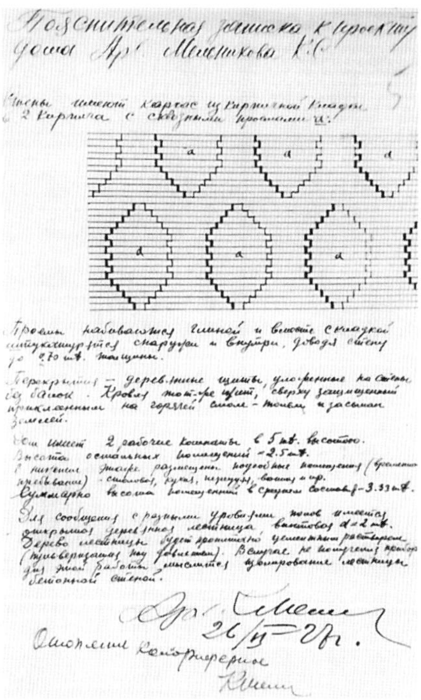

Gustav Klutsis, »The Russia of the NEP will give rise to a socialist Russia (Lenin)«, ca. 1922

Melnikov's description of his wall system, 1927

thaw period, to which Stalin soon put an end, was probably the only phase in the history of the Soviet Union during which an undertaking as fundamentally individual in nature as the building of a private home could be envisaged, yet even during this period it was anything but simple. Beside other problems there was a shortage of building materials. There was no question of using concrete or metal, and what was available – brick and wood – was also in short supply. Use of the kind of trained craftsmen that would have been needed for higher-quality work was reserved for public building projects, so that Melnikov had to rely on unskilled construction labourers, peasants who had moved to town and found employment doing odd jobs, people familiar with the rural construction methods of their native villages – which perhaps fitted in with Melnikov's intentions since in many ways his house, for all its unusual features, owes a great deal more to such rural tradition than to the avant-garde ideas of his time.

Necessity is the mother of invention: for his house, Melnikov devised both a geometry and a construction that, while they sprang from scarcity and limitation, in their elegance and sophistication show nothing of this, indeed, even seem to use these limitations effortlessly to their advantage.

Even tracing the form of the building can be accomplished quite simply – all you need is two pegs and a string. Let me refer briefly to the statical advantages of cylindrical buildings (the grain elevators mentioned previously owe their form to such considerations, of course); however, they are closely related to the most interesting aspect in this context, i.e., the construction of the outside walls. These are made of brick. Brick construction is one of the oldest traditions in architecture: the earliest known examples were excavated in Jericho and are just under 10,000 years old. Its techniques, too, may be described as archaic; no new inventions can be expected here, at least in a traditional context of building construction.

Melnikov, however, manages to do just that. His procedure is quite simple. He spans his openings by having the

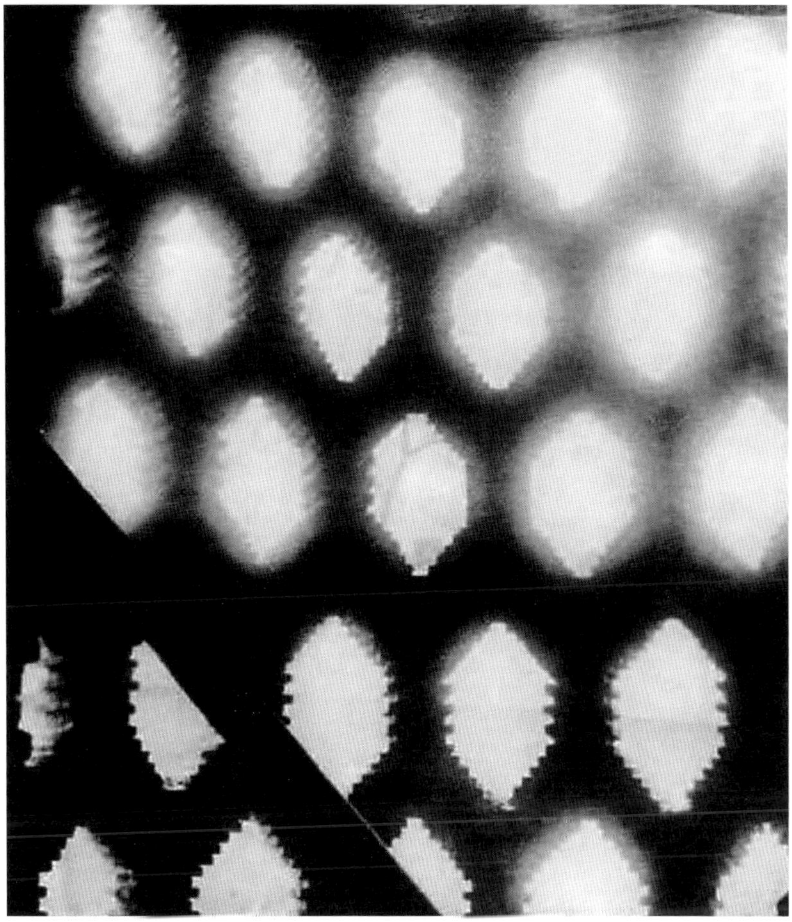

bricks of his block bond jut out by a quarter brick in every layer. He can thus do without complicated lintels, and also needs no formwork, only a model made of laths to ensure the regularity of the shape. To the same extent, he has the bricks recede in the next row of windows, so that he does not obtain a horizontal balustrade, but a v-shaped lower termination of his openings, a mirror image of the lintels. This once again may be traced back to late Baroque concepts, for instance, the windows of Dominikus Zimmermann and their relation to the wall they are set into. The staggering of the rows of windows thus follows automatically – as, of course, in Melnikov's organic structure everything seems to follow automatically, as it were.

A simpler, more economical and more obvious construction cannot be imagined. Its greatest economic advantage

The house under construction, 1927

Window and altar profiles by Dominikus Zimmermann: Kösingen (high altar) 1720, Günzburg 1736, Wies 1744 after Bauer / von der Mülbe 1985

is that it saves building material – in fact, not only are the window openings produced in this way, but the entire walls of both cylinders. Windows were installed in openings that were to remain, while the other ones were filled in with clay and rubble. – At this point it is important to remember that the economic situation of the Soviet Union toward the end of the 1920s was impacted by a shortage of goods and rationing, whereas labour was cheap. Therefore the Melnikov House could be built very economically (32,000 rubles, a fact that is commended by contemporary critics), and he proposed his wall system for larger public housing schemes.

It really is completely new – Melnikov's original contribution, unprecedented in the history of brick construction: He dissolves the wall – which otherwise appears either as a pure, though perhaps decorated surface, or is stabilised and subdivided by pilaster strips, i.e., linear elements – to create a structure where neither the vertical nor the horizontal nor the diagonal is predominant. The structure of the Melnikov wall system cannot be separated from its apertures – we must even go to such lengths as to regard the apertures as a structural characteristic of the wall, not only aesthetically but actually constructionally speaking, in perfect harmony with the material and the fabrication. Yet Melnikov's intentions can by no means be limited to the construction and its undeniable elegance – elegance in this case not in aesthetic terms, but in the sense of a constructional economy. The impression conveyed by this wall or in fact by this room is utterly overwhelming, and it is scarcely possible to figure out the reason for this: Is it the relation of the light to the space, or of the light to the substance of the wall, or that of the surface to the structure, or the solidity of the way the space is demarcated, or a perhaps subliminal tendency toward dematerialisation?

Here too we find a variety of factors to which the the character of the room could be traced back, each of them with the capability to provide a basic idea for the whole which can at least be tentatively ascribed – construction, configu-

← Melnikov's wall system

Foundation work, 1927

Melnikov with Anna Gavrilowna at the construction site, 1927

Ceiling construction. Top right: the head of Mikhail Vasilevich Gusev, whose friendship with Melnikov began in his childhood, and who supervised the construction

Alexander Rodchenko, Melnikov's house during plastering

ration, light, materiality, mass, proportion, dimension, etc. – yet such efforts will hardly yield more than partial success. Rather, all of these elements were developed to form a consistent entity, organic as it were, with one thing constantly dependent on another, simultaneous and without hierarchy, imagined concurrently, where each individual relation can certainly be regarded as the superordinated idea and backbone of the whole, yet always only on a trial basis, valid only for the current angle of vision, never claiming to be anything but provisionally valid.

Even the less spectacular aspects of the construction deserve closer attention. For instance, when it came to the wooden ceilings, Melnikov had to cope with spans of up to 9 metres, a less than simple undertaking. He solves this with the aid of a beam-and-girder construction, which he again assembles, using the least material, from slender, commercially available planks, without using any metal parts other than nails – the whole thing again very simply and completely produced on the construction site.

At this point we may wonder how to judge Melnikov's constructions. There can be no doubt that we are dealing with extraordinary achievements: Both in the case of the wall as well as of the ceilings, we are looking at exemplary innovations, which are extremely simple to boot. We must not forget the latter fact, since it points to something unique, a special path in modern architecture: we are facing a combination of totally new inventions here – technical as well as aesthetic – with completely traditional methods that are rooted in rural construction techniques, and traditional images as well. What is special about the Melnikov House is that it makes none of this explicit: the novelty does not display an avant-garde attitude, nor does the building's construction evoke archaism, and by no means does this result in a collision, a break used to stage a conflict, a tension. The opposite is true: no contradiction can be observed, it is all consistently contemporaneous, each aspect merges completely into the other. The effect is also totally in accordance with this: we experience the house both as something quite unusual, eternally new as it were, but also as something strangely familiar that we have known for a long time. The impossible and unresolvable consistency of the unaccustomed and of the familiar – perhaps this is the secret reason for the exceptionally strong, very precise and yet so elusive impression left by the house.

So we cannot choose the easy answer and explain everything simply, for instance, by the constraints under which the construction of the house took place. Nor is it very helpful to speak of a coincidence of fortunate circumstances. We could argue that this is genius, a term now frowned upon – we might speak not of Melnikov as a genius, but of Melnikov's ingenuity – and lastly we believe that in this enigmatic consistency we can see the manifestation of genuinely architectonic thinking and of the ›architectonic‹ we outlined above, the principle inherent in architecture. This is also reflected in the fact that Melnikov's house very precisely declares its position on the basic aspects of architecture, and if it does not answer complex theoretical questions it at least asks them, or rather: prompts us to ask them. It does not do so in a way that could be conclusively translated into language; rather, the medium is architecture itself, the building, which does not represent or formulate the facts, complexes, relations, but comprises them.

With this in mind the house should be regarded as a sign – as an object that combines complex relations into the consistency of the sign, capable of provoking a multitude of questions which, however, do not adhere to it, but roll off it as it were – as from the smooth, white surface of Valéry's *objet ambigu.*

Of course, it is quite indisputable that Melnikov's buildings and projects are highly symbolic. In some cases we have statements he made to that effect, which, however, one does not always have to be willing to take as the whole truth – frequently such a decoding of the signs is accompanied by a sense of embarrassment at the banality of the signified that

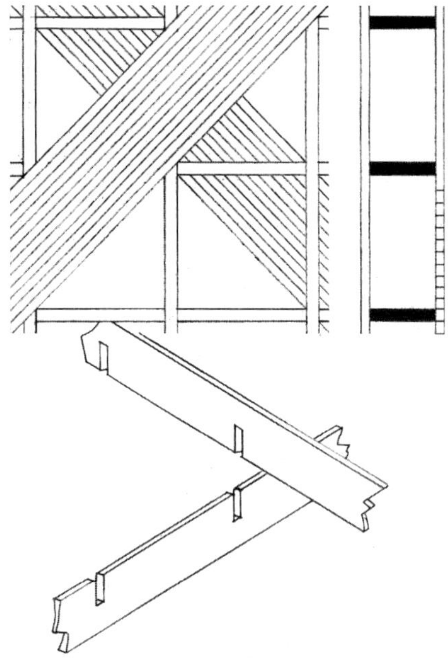

Diagram of ceiling construction

Palace of the Soviets, Moscow (CE), 1933, perspective and explanatory drawing

now becomes apparent. Thus in 1933 he says regarding his competition design for the Palace of the Soviets that it symbolises the struggle between old and new architectural forms – the triumph of the new forms is represented in the ever-developing form of the flower, while the surpassed old forms are embodied in the static, closed form of the pyramid. But this interpretation in terms of a rhetorical *architecture parlante* too obviously reveals the vagueness of the idea for us to be able really to take it at face value – the building itself at any rate speaks of far more complex circumstances.

What Melnikov really had to offer in his concern with the semiotic character and symbolism of architecture, and what might have developed had he not been prematurely cut off from all opportunities can be judged from the last buildings he implemented, two garages, projects in which according to his own statements he worked only on the design of the exterior; his colleague Kurochkin was responsible for the buildings themselves, as Melnikov emphasised.

At first the Intourist Garage. We are already familiar with its perspective refinements – let us now look at its semiotics. It turns out to be a virtually exemplary representative of ›speaking architecture‹ – almost blatantly it seems to be trying to represent the shape of a car and its individual parts. Not only is everything present: radiator mascot, mudguard, bumper, ventilation flaps, windscreen, wheel – everything is also where it belongs.

Cars particularly interested Melnikov, which should doubtless be viewed not least in the context of newly emerged architectural parameters of perception, a hitherto undreamt-of dynamism, a type of perspective set in motion that was previously unknown.

Decades later, what he most clearly remembers about Corbusier, who chauffeured him around Paris for a week to show him the latest buildings, is not so much the architecture as the fact that Corbusier owned a car. Then why shouldn't he put up a memorial to the car and create a building in its image – Lequeu's cowshed, showing up in the cul-

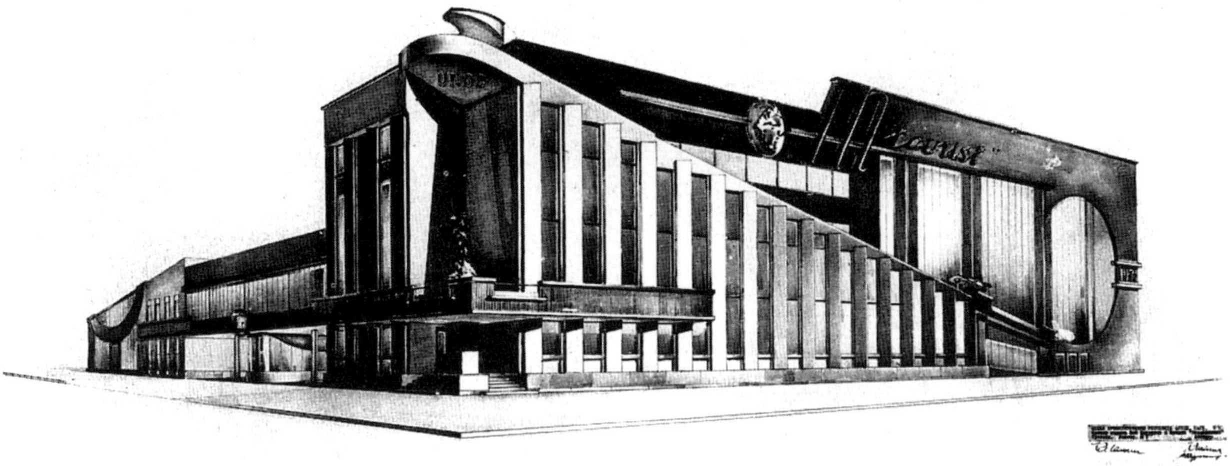

tural revolution? But let's not rush things though: We see nothing here that isn't already familiar to us from the context of Melnikov's architecture, or that couldn't be connected to familiar elements of a general architectural canon. Thus in the radiator mascot we rediscover the geometry of the staircase of his house, while the diagonal of the mudguard is omnipresent in all his buildings, the circle is his favourite form, the ventilation flaps as a reinterpretation of pilasters anything but unfamiliar, the bumper a simple balustrade.

The narrative element, too, with the model-like sculptural representation of a sports or race car tackling the mountain slope of the diagonal is nothing new: Since the Atlantes of the first Paris garage project, sculptural-representational elements have been increasingly making their way into the designs, and of course we have also frequently come across tautological décor in form of a scaled-down repetition of the overall shape.

In other words, it is equally true that this façade as a pictorial representation of a car is intended to be a conglomerate of established architectural elements, thus identifying its image as architecture. Accordingly we cannot be content with merely seeing Lequeu's cowshed in the Intourist Garage – if nothing else, because the two semiotic references, car and building, while they can be mapped upon each other, are nevertheless separated in a very precise, analytical

Intourist Garage, Moscow, 1934-36, perspektive view

Hispano Suiza R6C Speedster, 1930

Intourist Garage, view

Jean-Jacques Lequeu, »L'étable à vache tournée au midi [...]«, ca. 1800

Gosplan Garage, Moscow, 1934-36, condition in 2013

way. While the car, composed of architectural elements, is projected on the flat surface of the façade as a graphic image, the building immediately loses its imaging character, – which it owes to extra-architectonic elements – when it is revealed as a three-dimensional object, namely at the corner, and is now a genuine architectural structure – though perhaps here it should also be regarded as such in a representational way. In other words, we are dealing with somewhat complicated relationships, between two- and three-dimensionality, icon, representation, and the object as such; here we have Melnikov's complex contribution to an otherwise consistently avoided topic, i.e., to the systematics of the façade and to its theory.

Though the relationships are complicated, everything about the Intourist façade is derivable, identifiable, though not without ambivalences. That is not the case with the other one of Melnikov's last built works, developed concurrently – the garage for GosPlan, the State Planning Commission of the USSR. Here too Kurochkin was responsible for the entire complex; it is hard to tell the extent of Melnikov's influence on the design. Still, his authorship is undisputed for the large round ›window element‹ that projects from the elongated low garage hall next to the administration building – it remains to be seen whether it is true that a second one was planned at the opposite end.

This object is extremely puzzling. We have no credible clue to its function: what is its purpose, with this form, at this size? We cannot, in fact, discern a purpose from which form and size could be derived and which would be capable of justifying both. The whole thing leaves us baffled, we cannot read it. At the same time it undeniably seems to be a sign – only: what does it signify?

Sometimes it is taken for the image of a headlight – that would to some extent fit with the theme of the car; the light and illumination motifs could also be associated with the window, and at a pinch we could make up a connection to the sun worship practised by Melnikov and generally in the

Gosplan Garage, ca. 1936
anonymous photography
© The Schusev State Museum of Architecture, Moscow, 2015.

1920s and '30s – yet this interpretation, as dubious as it is banal, unquestionably falls short and can hardly be reconciled with the immense three-dimensional quality and architectural originality we see before us here.

Thus while the object gives no useful clue to a reference that would compellingly allow us to receive it as an icon or representation, the form also does not allow us to reach a definite conclusion as to its genesis. It is certainly not as if the circle were clearly the geometrical figure dependent from which the form then developed: rather, this circular form is quite clearly revealed to be not the cause, but the consequence, the result of an action, namely, the wrapping of a strip or a ribbon. Yet even if we disregard the three-dimensional components that do not quite seem to fit into this nar-

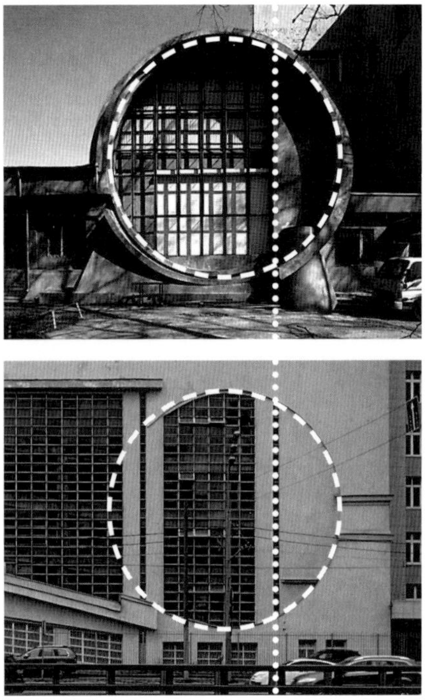

Gosplan and Intourist garages, geometric conformities

rative of how the form came about, the whole thing does not work. What we see before us cannot be unrolled, and neither can it be recreated from one or several ribbons, and thus unravelled: if we try to follow the edges, we get lost in paralogisms, in aporias. We must resign ourselves to the fact that Melnikov's object also does not admit a conclusive narrative of how it was formed.

Only as an architectonic object does it have validity; its indubitable consistency is accessible only if we regard it as such: It can be derived neither from an image, nor from a form, nor with regard to a structure or a function.

That means, of course, that it should also be completely stripped of all significance. Yet its character as a sign can scarcely be questioned – other than a sign, what would be left after eliminating everything else? At most it would be interpreted as an architectonic object in and of itself. Perhaps we can find a key in such a speculative assumption: a key that will make it possible for us to understand Melnikov's last work as a radical, pointed emphasis of the architectonic.

As an architectonic object in and of itself it would coincide with itself in its inevitable and fundamentally exclusive character as a sign, and could thus not be deciphered, only identified, referring to nothing but itself, and would thus be a perfect sign, precisely because of its seemingly absurd dissolution – as a sign of architecture per se, or rather: of the architectonic.

Thus the two last works conceptually mark out the territory of the semiotic nature of architecture: while both of them are signs, one of them is to be taken as a representation in each of its parts (even where it refers to nothing but architecture and thus represents the latter), whereas the other is to be taken only as the thing-in-itself. That they are intended to be programmatic counterparts is indicated by the exact correspondence of the division of both circles into open and closed surfaces, despite all explicit differences in the coding of components, relations and references.

How, then, should Melnikov's house be read as a sign? – One possible indication may be its designation. In a late text, in which he speaks of its meaning as a gesture, he refers to the inscription above the large window of the living room: ›KONSTANTIN MELNIKOV ARCHITECT‹. Not surprisingly, this aroused the criticism of his contemporaries, if nothing else. The inscription has to be be regarded as a prominent signature, and we must remember that his self-image as an artist was based on early experiences as a painter and that the signatures on his paintings, and on his architectural drawings, are always unmistakably striking and very impressive.

Street front with inscription

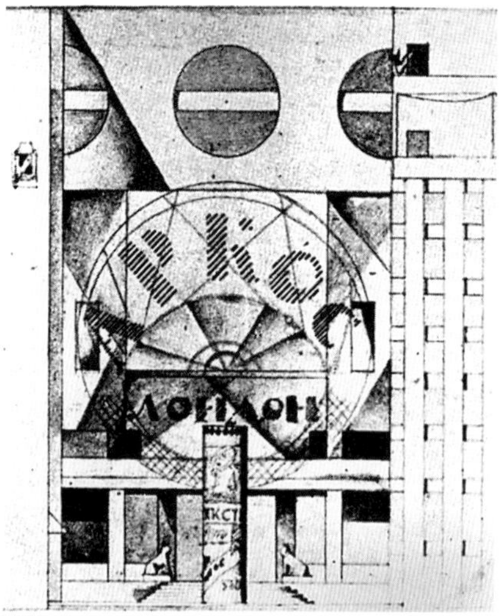

Administration building for the Arcos Foreign Trade Company, Moscow (CE), 1924

Kiosk, Exposition des Artistes Décorateurs, Paris 1925

Bakhmetevsky Bus Garage Moscow 1926

In many of his buildings inscriptions have an important role, as an essential and basically architectonic element. In addition to their aesthetic potential, which Melnikov explored in a masterly fashion, they also played a significant part in disengaging from traditional forms of architectonic iconography: no image, no architectonic décor, only the building itself and the inscription associated with it are there to communicate meaning. Here the inscription assumes iconographic functions, and this may be the reason for the occasional peculiar tautological or pleonastic association of inscription and building – writing ›club‹ in large letters on a club building about whose function there can hardly be any doubt is a little like writing ›vat‹ on a vat.

Let us consider the idea that it is precisely such semantic duplication that aims at the sign character of architecture itself, at architecture's identity as a conveyor of meaning beyond typology. We must remember that Melnikov is consistently opposed to anything that has to do with typology. That his buildings must be regarded as emblematic is beyond doubt, yet he painstakingly avoids any misunderstanding of these references as typological – quite the contrary, in their constant ambivalence they must be understood as being explicitly directed against any type of typology and typification.

Thus the signature on Melnikov's house must at all events be regarded as a sign, inasmuch as it refers to something. As the conveyor of this inscription, the house itself is designated in reference to its emblematic character, and it is the text itself that provides the clue: the individuality and person of the architect, represented in the name, not separated and inseparable from his work. If that is true, then the sign that is the house explicitly denotes architecture itself, and proclaims its position here: in denying any typological identification, it recognises architecture as an autonomous art, and defines itself and thus also the architectonic work of art as such, linked to the name and profession of the architect, as the work of an artist.

BIBLIOGRAPHICAL REFERENCES

BAUER, HERMANN and **ANNA; VON DER MÜLBE, WOLF-CHRISTIAN,** *Johann Baptist und Dominikus Zimmermann*, Regensburg 1985.

BALDEWEG, JUAN NAVARRO; JAQUE, ANDRÉS, *Konstantin Melnikov. Aparcamiento para 1000 autos, 2ª variante*, Madrid 2004.

BARUCKI, TADEUSZ, *Konstanty Mielnikow*, Warsaw 1981.

BREUER, DAVID (ed.), *Baumeister der Revolution*, Essen 2011.

CHAN-MAGOMEDOV, SELIM OMAROVIČ, *Architektor Konstantin Mel'nikov (pionery sovetskoj architektury)*, Moscow 1981.

— *Pioniere der sowjetischen Architektur. Der Weg zur neuen sowjetischen Architektur in den zwanziger und zu Beginn der dreißiger Jahre*, Vienna 1983. Engl.: *Pioneers of Soviet architecture: the search for new solutions in the 1920s and 1930s*, New York NY 1987.

— *Krivoarbatskiĭ pereulok, 10*, Moscow 1984.

— *Konstantin Mel'nikov*, Moscow 1990.

CHATWIN, BRUCE, *What am I doing here*, London 1990.

DE MAGISTRIS, ALESSANDRO, *La casa cilindrica di Konstantin Mel'nikov. 1927-1929*, Turin 1998.

FOSSO, MARIO (ed.), *Konstantin S. Mel'nikov and the construction of Moscow*, Milan 2000.

GROYS, BORIS, *Über das Neue. Versuch einer Kulturökonomie*, Munich, Vienna 1992. Engl.: *On the new*, Brooklyn NY 2014.

HEIDEGGER, MARTIN, *Die Kunst und der Raum*, St. Gallen 1969. Engl.: *Art and Space*, The Hague 1973.

LISSITZKY, EL, *Rußland. Die Rekonstruktion der Architektur in der Sowjetunion*, Wien 1930. Reprint as *1929 Rußland: Architektur für eine Weltrevolution*, Berlin, Frankfurt/M., Vienna 1965. Engl.: *Russia: an architecture for world revolution*, Cambridge MA, 1970.

MIDDLETON, ROBIN; WATKIN, DAVID J., *Architektur der Neuzeit*, Stuttgart 1977.

MULLAGILDIN, RISHAT (ed.), *Architecture of Konstantin Melnikov. 1920s-1930s*, Tokyo 2002.

PALLASMAA, JUHANI; GOZAK, ANDREI, *The Melnikov house, Moscow (1927-1929)*, London 1996.

STARR, S. FREDERICK, *Melnikov. Solo architect in a mass society*, Princeton NJ 1978.

— *K. Mel'nikov. Le pavillon soviétique – Paris 1925*, Paris 1981

WORTMANNN, ARTHUR (ed.), *Melnikov. The Muscles of Invention*, Rotterdam 1990.

LIST OF ILLUSTRATIONS

The illustrations were reproduced with friendly permission of the following authors or taken from the following publications (numbering on the respective pages from top to bottom or clockwise, beginning top left):

Melnikov's drawings from Chan-Magomedov 1990, Pallasmaa/Gozak 1996, Starr 1978, Starr 1981.

Ground plans and sectional view based on various drawings by Melnikov and plans published by Pallasmaa/Gozak 1996, redrawn by the author.

Isometric drawing p. 51 by Friedrich Barth.

Melnikov quotations after Chan-Magomedov 1983 and Mullagildin 2002.